JADEN CROSS

C#9 Clean Architecture with .NET 5

Contents

Introduction: Why Clean Architecture Matters

Software development has evolved significantly over the years, and as technology advances, the complexity of software systems grows. Developers and architects face new challenges in building applications that not only function as intended but also remain maintainable, scalable, and adaptable to change. This is where clean architecture comes into play, offering a blueprint for developing software solutions that meet these needs. In this section, we'll explore the significance of clean architecture, why it's essential, and how it can transform the way you approach software development.

The Growing Complexity of Modern Software

As applications grow in size and complexity, developers often find themselves struggling to manage codebases that become increasingly unmanageable. Features are added, bugs are fixed, and integrations are built, all of which contribute to a codebase that, if not properly structured, can become tangled and difficult to maintain. Over time, the software's architecture may degrade, resulting in a phenomenon commonly known as "spaghetti code," where interdependencies make even minor changes risky and expensive.

Traditional architectural patterns, such as the monolithic and layered architectures, have served their purposes, but they often fail to provide the flexibility needed in today's development environments. With the advent of microservices, cloud computing, and agile methodologies, there's a growing need for architectures that are resilient, modular, and easy to evolve. Clean architecture addresses these challenges by emphasizing principles that keep codebases manageable, maintainable, and adaptable.

What Is Clean Architecture?

Clean architecture is an architectural pattern introduced by Robert C. Martin (commonly known as Uncle Bob) to address the complexities associated with modern software development. It builds on the principles of earlier architectural patterns like hexagonal architecture (also known as ports and adapters) and onion architecture, extending them to create a more cohesive and maintainable system.

At its core, clean architecture divides an application into layers, each with distinct responsibilities. The idea is to separate the business logic, application logic, and infrastructure logic to ensure that changes in one area have minimal impact on others. This separation of concerns leads to a modular codebase where individual components can be developed, tested, and maintained independently.

A key principle of clean architecture is dependency inversion, which dictates that higher-level modules should not depend on lower-level modules. Instead, both should depend on abstractions. This inversion of control decouples the business logic from the technical details, making it easier to change technologies or infrastructure without affecting the core application logic.

The Principles of Clean Architecture

To fully understand why clean architecture matters, it's crucial to grasp the principles that underpin it. These principles are designed to promote software development practices that result in flexible, scalable, and maintainable code:

1. **Separation of Concerns**: Clean architecture promotes the division of an application into layers, each with a distinct role. This separation ensures that concerns like business logic, user interface, and data access are isolated, making it easier to develop, test, and maintain each part independently.

2. **Dependency Inversion**: One of the most important principles of clean architecture is dependency inversion, which reverses traditional dependencies. Instead of high-level modules depending on low-level modules (e.g., business logic depending on data access), they both depend on abstractions. This reduces the coupling between components and enhances flexibility.

3. **Testability**: By structuring code in a way that isolates business logic from infrastructure and user interfaces, clean architecture makes it easier to write unit tests. Components can be tested independently, leading to a robust and reliable application.

4. **Portability and Flexibility**: With clean architecture, it's possible to change technologies or frameworks with minimal impact on the core business logic. Whether it's swapping a database technology or integrating a new front-end framework, clean architecture supports these changes with minimal disruption.

5. **Resilience and Scalability**: Applications built using clean architecture are more resilient and scalable, as the modular design allows individual components to be optimized, replaced, or scaled without affecting the entire system.

Why Developers and Architects Should Embrace Clean Architecture

The real value of clean architecture lies in its ability to solve some of the most common problems developers face. By providing a structured approach to building software, clean architecture empowers developers and architects to design systems that are not only functional but also easy to manage and extend. Below are some key benefits:

1. **Improved Maintainability**: As software evolves, maintenance becomes a critical concern. Clean architecture makes it easier to navigate and understand code, reducing the effort needed for bug fixes and feature enhancements.

2. **Ease of Testing**: Testing is an integral part of software development. Clean architecture, with its emphasis on modularity and separation of

concerns, enables developers to isolate components, making it easier to write unit tests and integration tests. This results in a more reliable application and reduces the risk of regressions.

3. **Adaptability to Change**: In the fast-paced world of technology, frameworks and tools evolve rapidly. Applications designed with clean architecture can easily adapt to these changes because the core business logic is decoupled from the technical implementations. This adaptability ensures that your application can evolve without major rewrites, saving time and resources.

4. **Scalability**: As applications grow in complexity, the need to scale becomes inevitable. Clean architecture provides the modularity required to scale individual components independently. Whether you need to scale your data access layer, add new features, or optimize your API endpoints, clean architecture allows you to do so with minimal impact on the overall system.

5. **Clear Communication and Collaboration**: Clean architecture provides a common language and structure for developers and architects, making it easier to collaborate on projects. By following a consistent architectural pattern, teams can work more effectively, and new team members can onboard quickly without having to decipher complex, undocumented codebases.

Applying Clean Architecture in Real-World Scenarios

To understand the impact of clean architecture, it's important to consider how it applies in real-world software development scenarios:

- **Enterprise Applications**: In large organizations, software systems often integrate with multiple databases, APIs, and user interfaces. Clean architecture provides the flexibility needed to manage these complexities while keeping the core business logic intact. Changes to any external dependencies, such as switching databases or APIs, can be managed with minimal changes to the application's core.

- **Microservices and Cloud-Native Applications**: Clean architecture is particularly well-suited for microservices and cloud-native architectures, where modularity and independence are crucial. By building microservices using clean architecture, developers can ensure that each service is isolated and can evolve independently without affecting others. This approach aligns well with cloud-native principles, where services must be resilient, scalable, and easily deployable.

- **Web and Mobile Applications**: For web and mobile development, clean architecture facilitates the separation of UI, business logic, and data access. This separation allows teams to build web and mobile applications using different frameworks or technologies while reusing the core business logic. For instance, the same application logic can be shared between an ASP.NET Core web application and a Xamarin mobile application, reducing development time and increasing consistency.

Why .NET 5 and C#9 Are Ideal for Clean Architecture

With the release of .NET 5 and C#9, Microsoft has provided a unified platform and a set of powerful features that align well with clean architecture principles. Let's explore why these technologies are a perfect fit:

- **Unified Platform**: .NET 5 brings together various frameworks (e.g., .NET Core, ASP.NET, Xamarin) into a single platform, making it easier to build applications with a consistent architecture across different domains (web, desktop, mobile). This unification simplifies the development process and aligns with the modular approach of clean architecture.

- **C#9 Features**: C#9 introduces several features, such as records, pattern matching enhancements, and top-level programs, that enhance the development experience when building clean architecture solutions. For instance, records allow for immutable data structures that fit well with domain models, and pattern matching simplifies complex logic without compromising readability.

- **Performance and Flexibility**: .NET 5's performance optimizations and support for asynchronous programming make it a powerful platform for building scalable applications. Combined with clean architecture, developers can design systems that handle high loads efficiently while maintaining clean, testable code.

Conclusion

Clean architecture is not just another architectural pattern; it's a transformative approach to software development that can significantly enhance the quality, maintainability, and scalability of your applications. By embracing the principles of clean architecture and leveraging the features of .NET 5 and C#9, you can build software systems that are resilient, flexible, and ready for the future. This book will guide you through each step of implementing clean architecture, providing practical examples and real-world scenarios to ensure you can apply these concepts effectively in your own projects.

As we proceed, we'll explore each layer of clean architecture in detail, demonstrating how to build applications that stand the test of time. Whether you're an experienced developer looking to deepen your architectural skills or a software architect seeking a practical guide, this book will equip you with the knowledge and tools needed to master clean architecture with .NET 5 and C#9.

Setting Up Your Development Environment

The foundation of any successful software project lies in a well-configured development environment. A robust and streamlined setup not only simplifies the development process but also ensures consistency across different machines and among team members. This chapter will guide you through setting up the necessary tools and frameworks for building applications with C#9 and .NET 5, specifically tailored for clean architecture. We'll cover everything from the installation of the required software to configuring your project to align with clean architectural principles.

Essential Software and Tools

Before diving into the specifics of project setup, let's first ensure that all necessary tools and software are installed on your development machine. Here's what you'll need:

1. **Visual Studio 2019 or Later**: Visual Studio is a powerful IDE that supports .NET development, providing extensive features for coding, debugging, and testing. Ensure you have Visual Studio 2019 or a later version installed to take advantage of all the features relevant to .NET 5 and C#9.

2. **.NET 5 SDK**: The Software Development Kit (SDK) includes everything needed to develop and run .NET 5 applications. It comes with the

runtime for running apps and a set of libraries and APIs for building them.

3. **SQL Server Express**: For database operations, SQL Server Express is a free, lightweight, and easy-to-install version of Microsoft SQL Server. This will be used to manage the relational data within our applications.

4. **Git**: Version control is crucial for any project. Git will help manage source code history and collaborate with other developers. Ensure Git is installed and configured on your machine.

5. **Postman**: This tool is essential for testing APIs. Postman allows you to design, mock, debug, automatically test, document, and monitor your APIs.

6. **Docker** (optional): For those planning to containerize their applications, Docker provides a standardized unit of software, packaging up code and all its dependencies so the application runs quickly and reliably from one computing environment to another.

Installing Visual Studio and .NET 5 SDK

Follow these steps to install Visual Studio and the .NET 5 SDK:

1. **Download Visual Studio**: Go to the Visual Studio downloads page and select the edition that fits your needs (Community, Professional, or Enterprise). The Community version is free and sufficient for most development needs.

2. **Customize Installation**: During the installation process, select the ".NET desktop development" workload, which includes all necessary components for developing with .NET and C#. Ensure that the "ASP.NET and web development" workload is also selected to work with web applications.

3. **Install .NET 5 SDK**: While Visual Studio 2019 and later typically include the .NET 5 SDK, it's a good practice to verify and install the latest version. You can download it from the .NET 5 official site. Follow the installation instructions provided on the website.

Configuring Your Development Environment

Once the installations are complete, the next step is to configure your environment to support clean architecture:

- **Creating a Solution Structure**: Open Visual Studio and create a new solution. Name it according to your project. For clean architecture, you'll typically organize your solution into at least four projects:
- Domain: Contains all entities, enums, exceptions, interfaces, types, and logic specific to the domain layer.
- Application: Contains all application logic. It depends on the domain layer but has no dependencies on any external layers such as Infrastructure or Presentation.
- Infrastructure: Contains classes for accessing external resources such as file systems, web services, SMTP, and SQL databases.
- Presentation: This could be an ASP.NET Core Web API project or any other form of application that interacts with the user.
- **Setting Up Dependency Management**: Clean architecture relies on dependencies being correctly managed. Use Visual Studio's built-in NuGet package manager to add and manage dependencies. For instance, you might add Entity Framework Core to the Infrastructure project for ORM functionality.
- **Version Control Integration**: Initialize a Git repository in your solution directory. Visual Studio has built-in support for Git, allowing you to manage version control directly within the IDE. Commit your initial project structure to Git to start tracking changes.
- **Database Configuration**: Connect your application to SQL Server Express by adding the connection string in the appsettings.json file of your Presentation project. Use Entity Framework Core migrations to set up and manage your database schema effectively.
- **API Testing Setup**: Configure Postman by creating a new collection for your project. As you build out your APIs in the Presentation layer, use Postman to test them, ensuring they function as expected before integration with frontend applications or other services.

- **Docker Configuration** (optional): If using Docker, add a Dockerfile to your Presentation project to containerize your application. This involves defining the base image, setting up the environment, copying your published application into the container, and configuring the entry point.

Finalizing Your Setup

With your development environment set up, you're now ready to start building applications using clean architecture. This setup not only facilitates development but also ensures that your project remains organized and maintainable. It supports the principles of clean architecture by separating concerns, managing dependencies effectively, and allowing for easy expansion and testing.

C#9 and .NET 5: What's New and Why It Matters

The release of .NET 5 and C#9 introduced significant improvements and features that make application development faster, more efficient, and better suited to modern architectural patterns like clean architecture. .NET 5 represents Microsoft's shift to a unified platform, consolidating the previously separate .NET Core, .NET Framework, and Xamarin frameworks into a single ecosystem. This shift provides developers with a consistent development experience across various platforms, whether for web, desktop, mobile, or cloud applications. C#9, the language update accompanying .NET 5, brings with it syntax and structural improvements that enhance both code readability and functionality, making it ideal for clean, maintainable code.

In this chapter, we'll explore the new features in C#9 and .NET 5, explaining how each contributes to a clean, scalable, and efficient architecture.

The Unified Vision of .NET 5

Microsoft designed .NET 5 to unify the .NET ecosystem, breaking down the silos between .NET Framework, .NET Core, and Xamarin. This unified platform allows developers to use the same base libraries, APIs, and runtime across various application types and operating systems, including Windows, macOS, and Linux. This vision of a "One .NET" ecosystem has substantial benefits for developers working with clean architecture:

11

1. **Consistency Across Platforms**: A unified platform means developers can use the same codebase, libraries, and development environment, regardless of the target platform. This consistency aligns perfectly with clean architecture, where modular design and platform independence are essential.

2. **Improved Performance**: .NET 5 includes a range of performance enhancements. For example, garbage collection and runtime optimizations make applications run faster and more efficiently. This performance improvement is critical for scalable applications where responsiveness and low latency are necessary.

3. **Enhanced Support for Cloud and Microservices**: With .NET 5, applications are better suited for cloud environments. For instance, improvements in ASP.NET Core enable developers to create lightweight APIs and services optimized for microservice architectures. This support for cloud-native design is a powerful complement to clean architecture principles.

New Features in C#9: Streamlining Code for Clean Architecture

C#9 introduces several features that support the principles of clean architecture by promoting code clarity, immutability, and separation of concerns. Let's take a closer look at these features and how they apply to clean architecture.

- **Records: A New Way to Define Data Models**
- Records are one of the most anticipated features in C#9, offering a simple and concise way to define data models that are immutable by default. Traditional classes are mutable, meaning their fields can change after object creation, which often leads to unexpected behaviors and bugs. In contrast, records make it easy to create immutable types, ensuring that data remains consistent throughout the application.

Example:

```
public record Customer(int Id, string Name, string Email);
```

In clean architecture, immutability is essential for entities and value objects within the core domain. Using records, you can represent these types without needing to worry about unwanted side effects caused by data changes. Records also support value-based equality, so two instances with the same values are considered equal, making them ideal for entities and identifiers within the core domain layer.

- **Init-Only Setters: Enforcing Immutability**
- Alongside records, C#9 introduces init-only properties, which allow properties to be set only during initialization. This means that after an object is created, its properties cannot be modified. Init-only setters are an excellent way to enforce immutability without using records.

Example:

```
public class Order
{
    public int Id { get; init; }
    public string Product { get; init; }
    public decimal Price { get; init; }
}
```

Init-only setters are especially useful in domain-driven design (DDD), where immutability helps prevent accidental changes to the state of domain entities. This feature ensures that once an entity is created, its state remains consistent, promoting reliability and reducing potential errors in complex applications.

- **Enhanced Pattern Matching: Simplifying Complex Logic**
- Pattern matching in C#9 has been expanded to include new capabilities like relational patterns, logical patterns, and type patterns, making it easier to handle complex conditional logic. In clean architecture, pattern matching can simplify code within application services, especially when

working with various types in business logic.

Example:

```
public decimal CalculateDiscount(object customer)
{
    return customer switch
    {
        GoldCustomer => 0.20m,
        SilverCustomer => 0.10m,
        BronzeCustomer => 0.05m,
        _ => 0.0m
    };
}
```

By eliminating nested if or switch statements, pattern matching improves code readability and reduces complexity, making the application logic easier to understand and maintain.

- **Top-Level Statements: Simplifying Entry Points**
- C#9 introduces top-level statements, allowing developers to write simpler, more concise entry points for applications. While this feature is primarily beneficial for small projects or educational code, it can streamline setup for lightweight services or scripts within a clean architecture setup.

Example:

```
using System;

Console.WriteLine("Welcome to the Clean Architecture App!");
```

Top-level statements reduce boilerplate code, especially in console applications, making it easier to focus on the core functionality without unnecessary setup code.

- **With-Expressions: Creating Modified Copies of Objects**
- With-expressions provide a simple way to create modified copies of an object without altering the original instance. This is particularly useful in clean architecture when working with immutable objects, where changes need to reflect a new state without directly modifying the existing instance.

Example:

```
var customer = new Customer("John", "Doe");
var updatedCustomer = customer with { LastName = "Smith" };
```

By promoting immutability, with-expressions help ensure that the application state remains consistent, preventing unintended side effects in domain and application layers.

- **Covariant Return Types: Enhancing Code Flexibility**
- Covariant return types allow derived classes to override methods and return more specific types than the return types defined in the base class. This feature provides flexibility and can enhance code readability, making it more intuitive when working with domain-specific models or services in clean architecture.

Example:

```
public class BaseEntity { }
public class User : BaseEntity { }

public abstract class Repository
{
    public virtual BaseEntity GetEntity() => new BaseEntity();
}

public class UserRepository : Repository
```

```
{
    public override User GetEntity() => new User();
}
```

Covariant return types make code more adaptable to specific requirements, improving the way inheritance is handled in complex architectures.

Performance Enhancements in .NET 5

.NET 5 includes several performance improvements that make it ideal for high-performance applications. Whether you're developing APIs, background services, or user-facing applications, these optimizations ensure faster response times and lower resource usage.

1. **Improved Garbage Collection**: .NET 5's garbage collector (GC) has been optimized to handle high-load scenarios with reduced latency, making applications more responsive.
2. **JIT (Just-In-Time) Compiler Enhancements**: The new JIT compiler in .NET 5 generates more efficient machine code, improving the runtime performance of applications.
3. **Better JSON Serialization**: JSON serialization is a critical part of many .NET applications, especially for APIs. .NET 5 improves serialization performance, reducing the time taken to serialize and deserialize JSON objects.
4. **HTTP/2 and gRPC Improvements**: .NET 5 includes enhanced support for HTTP/2 and gRPC, both of which are critical for microservices and high-performance APIs. These protocols provide better performance and lower latency for inter-service communication.
5. **Support for WebAssembly**: .NET 5 introduces support for WebAssembly, allowing developers to run .NET code in the browser. While this feature is still evolving, it opens new possibilities for building web applications with .NET.

Why These Features Matter for Clean Architecture

The features introduced in C#9 and .NET 5 align well with the principles of clean architecture. Here's how each of these benefits clean architecture specifically:

- **Immutability and Reliability**: With records, init-only setters, and with-expressions, you can create immutable data structures that are reliable and maintainable. These immutable structures are crucial in clean architecture, especially in domain-driven design, where consistency is key.
- **Code Readability and Maintenance**: Enhanced pattern matching, top-level statements, and covariant return types make the code more readable and maintainable, which are essential aspects of clean architecture. With less boilerplate code and more intuitive logic, developers can focus on the application's core functionality.
- **Modularity and Separation of Concerns**: The unified .NET 5 platform ensures that the application's core logic is isolated from specific platform dependencies, supporting clean architecture's emphasis on separation of concerns.
- **High Performance and Scalability**: Performance enhancements in .NET 5 ensure that applications remain responsive and can scale as needed. Clean architecture applications benefit from these improvements, as each layer can be optimized independently, enhancing the scalability of the overall system.

Understanding Clean Architecture Principles

C lean architecture is a powerful approach to designing software systems that emphasizes maintainability, flexibility, and separation of concerns. It builds upon foundational software design concepts to provide a structure where each part of the application has a well-defined role, minimizing dependencies between different layers. Clean architecture's principles are particularly beneficial as systems grow in complexity, making it easier to implement new features, maintain existing code, and scale applications as demands increase.

In this chapter, we will explore the key principles of clean architecture, how it organizes different layers within an application, and why each principle is critical for building robust, scalable software.

The Core Goals of Clean Architecture

At its heart, clean architecture seeks to achieve several core goals that address common challenges in software development:

1. **Maintainability**: As applications evolve, the ability to modify code without impacting other parts of the system becomes critical. Clean architecture makes code easy to understand and alter, which minimizes the risks associated with maintenance.

2. **Testability**: Testing is an integral part of modern development practices. Clean architecture supports unit and integration testing by isolating

different parts of the application, allowing developers to test components independently.

3. **Scalability**: For applications that need to scale, whether in terms of functionality or performance, clean architecture provides the modularity and structure necessary to expand without major rewrites or re-architecting.

4. **Independence of Frameworks**: By minimizing dependencies on specific frameworks or libraries, clean architecture ensures that applications are not tightly coupled to third-party code. This independence allows developers to switch frameworks or upgrade components with minimal impact.

5. **Adaptability**: The clean architecture approach makes it easier to accommodate changing requirements, whether it's a new feature, integration, or platform. The loosely coupled layers allow new elements to be added or existing ones to be modified without widespread changes to the codebase.

The Layers of Clean Architecture

Clean architecture organizes an application into layers, each with a clear role. By dividing an application into these distinct layers, clean architecture creates a separation of concerns that promotes modularity and maintainability. Let's break down each layer and its responsibilities.

The Domain Layer (Core): This is the innermost layer, often referred to as the "core" of the application. It contains the business logic and rules that define how the application behaves. Key components of this layer include:

- **Entities**: Represent the core business objects and encapsulate business rules.
- **Value Objects**: Hold data that represent concepts in the business domain.
- **Aggregates**: Group closely related entities, maintaining consistency within a business transaction.
- **Domain Services**: Capture logic that doesn't naturally belong to a specific entity.

- **Interfaces**: Define contracts that other layers must implement, without specifying how.
- The domain layer should be independent of other layers, meaning it doesn't know about or depend on any technical implementation details. Its only role is to contain the rules and policies of the application.

The Application Layer: This layer defines the use cases and interactions of the application. It orchestrates the flow of information between the domain layer and other layers, such as infrastructure or presentation. Components within this layer include:

- **Use Cases**: Also known as "application services," use cases define the specific actions or operations that can be performed. Each use case represents a specific function of the application, such as "place an order" or "generate a report."
- **Interfaces and Commands**: These define the structure of actions that can be taken, ensuring clear communication with other layers.
- **Mediators and Events**: Mediation patterns, such as the CQRS (Command Query Responsibility Segregation) pattern, can be implemented here to handle interactions.
- The application layer doesn't contain business rules itself but coordinates the application's workflow by making calls to the domain layer. It's independent of any external technologies and communicates only through defined interfaces.

The Infrastructure Layer: This layer implements the technical details of the application. It contains classes for data access, networking, file storage, and other external resources. Key components include:

- **Repositories**: Implement data access logic and communicate with a database, typically using an ORM (Object-Relational Mapping) tool like Entity Framework.
- **External Services**: Any service that the application interacts with, such

as external APIs, file systems, email services, and caching mechanisms.

- **Persistence and Integration Components**: Manage the infrastructure aspects of the application, making the required technical implementation available to the rest of the application through interfaces defined in the core layers.
- The infrastructure layer depends on the interfaces defined in the domain and application layers, fulfilling their contracts by providing technical implementations. This layer is responsible for the "plumbing" of the application, connecting it to the outside world.

The Presentation Layer: Also known as the "interface" layer, this layer contains the code that interacts with users, such as a web front end, mobile application, or desktop interface. Its responsibilities include:

- **Controllers and APIs**: Handle incoming requests and route them to the appropriate use cases or services.
- **UI Components**: Define the visual aspects of the application, such as HTML pages, CSS, JavaScript, or XAML files.
- **View Models**: Translate data from the application layer into formats suitable for display.
- The presentation layer depends on the application layer but should not contain business rules or interact directly with the domain layer. Its focus is on handling user input, managing interactions, and presenting data, with all business logic managed by the underlying layers.

Key Principles of Clean Architecture

To fully grasp the value of clean architecture, let's explore the specific principles that make it so effective:

1. **Separation of Concerns**: Each layer in clean architecture has a single responsibility, making it easier to modify one part without impacting others. This separation reduces dependencies and keeps each part of the codebase manageable and focused.

2. **Dependency Inversion Principle (DIP)**: At the heart of clean architecture is the dependency inversion principle, which dictates that higher-level modules should not depend on lower-level modules; instead, both should depend on abstractions. In clean architecture, this means that the domain and application layers define interfaces, while the infrastructure and presentation layers implement those interfaces. This inversion of dependencies creates a modular and loosely coupled structure, making it easier to change technical details without affecting the core application logic.

3. **Encapsulation of Business Logic**: In clean architecture, the business logic is isolated in the domain layer, encapsulating the core rules and policies of the application. This isolation means that changes to the business logic don't affect other layers, ensuring that the application remains stable and predictable.

4. **Testability**: By separating the business logic from infrastructure and presentation concerns, clean architecture makes it easier to write tests for individual components. The domain and application layers can be tested independently from the infrastructure layer, reducing the time and effort required to ensure code reliability.

5. **Framework Independence**: Clean architecture avoids dependencies on specific frameworks or libraries, making it possible to replace components with minimal impact on the rest of the system. This framework independence is crucial for applications that need to evolve over time, as it allows developers to adopt new technologies or platforms without extensive rewrites.

Why These Principles Matter for Real-World Applications

The principles of clean architecture are particularly valuable when applied to real-world projects, where the need for flexibility, scalability, and maintainability is constant:

- **Flexibility in Adapting to Change**: Clean architecture allows applications to adapt to new requirements without major restructuring.

Whether adding a new feature, integrating with a third-party service, or replacing a legacy component, clean architecture provides a framework where these changes are manageable and isolated.

- **Ease of Maintenance and Collaboration**: As software projects grow, the need for clear, maintainable code increases. Clean architecture's separation of concerns and modularity make it easier for teams to work together on complex projects, as each team can focus on a specific layer without impacting others.

- **Scalability for Growing Applications**: When building scalable systems, clean architecture ensures that each layer can grow independently. For example, an increase in database usage can be addressed in the infrastructure layer without affecting the core business logic. This separation enables more straightforward scalability, whether vertical or horizontal.

Applying Clean Architecture in Your Projects

Implementing clean architecture requires a clear understanding of each layer's role and a commitment to following the principles that ensure modularity and separation of concerns. Here are some practical tips for applying clean architecture principles in your projects:

1. **Define Clear Boundaries**: Identify the business rules, use cases, and technical dependencies for each layer. Avoid leaking implementation details from one layer into another, as this weakens the modular structure.

2. **Use Interfaces to Manage Dependencies**: Rely on interfaces in the core layers, such as the domain and application layers, to define contracts. The infrastructure and presentation layers should implement these interfaces, creating a clear dependency flow that adheres to the dependency inversion principle.

3. **Isolate the Core Domain Logic**: Ensure that the domain layer has no dependencies on external frameworks or libraries. This isolation keeps the core logic independent and prevents changes in external

dependencies from affecting the core functionality.

4. **Write Tests for Each Layer**: Test the domain and application layers independently, focusing on the business logic and use cases. Use integration tests to verify that the infrastructure and presentation layers function correctly when interacting with external resources.

5. **Document Your Architecture**: Use diagrams and clear documentation to describe the relationships between layers, dependencies, and interfaces. Documentation helps maintain consistency and allows new team members to understand the structure of the application quickly.

Building the Core Layer

The core layer is the heart of any clean architecture application. It contains the business rules, entities, and policies that define the core functionality of the software, independent of any technical frameworks or dependencies. This separation allows the core layer to be robust, maintainable, and easily adaptable to changes without being affected by external technologies or infrastructure.

In this chapter, we'll dive into the details of building the core layer in a clean architecture application. We'll explore the components of the core layer— entities, value objects, aggregates, and domain services— and understand how to use C#9 features to implement them effectively.

Key Concepts in the Core Layer

Before jumping into implementation, let's review some essential concepts in the core layer that help establish a clean and modular structure.

1. **Entities**: Represent core business objects with a unique identifier and encapsulate the application's business rules.
2. **Value Objects**: Immutable objects that represent specific business values but lack unique identifiers. They encapsulate values with meaning in the domain.
3. **Aggregates**: A cluster of entities and value objects that form a consistency boundary, where any changes are controlled by a root entity.
4. **Domain Services**: Stateless services that contain business logic which doesn't naturally belong within any entity.

Each of these components contributes to the overall integrity of the domain, helping to ensure that the application's core rules and policies remain consistent.

Setting Up the Core Layer Project Structure

To begin, create a new project within your solution named Core or Domain. This project will be the foundation of the core layer, containing all the business rules and logic. Organize the folder structure to separate different domain concepts:

- **Entities**: A folder for business entities (e.g., Customer, Order).
- **ValueObjects**: A folder for any value objects (e.g., Money, Address).
- **Aggregates**: A folder for aggregates that group related entities.
- **Interfaces**: A folder to define interfaces for services.
- **Services**: A folder for domain services that contain business logic.

By organizing the core layer this way, each component remains easy to find and manage, helping maintain a clear separation of concerns.

Implementing Entities

Entities are central to the domain model, representing the business objects with unique identifiers. Each entity encapsulates the rules and behaviors that govern its state, ensuring that only valid operations are allowed.

Defining an Entity Base Class

Start by creating a base class for entities. This base class can handle common entity properties and methods, such as an Id and equality checks. Using C#9's record feature, we can enforce immutability in entities where appropriate.

Example: Base Entity

```
public abstract class Entity
{
    public int Id { get; protected set; }
```

```
public override bool Equals(object obj)
{
    if (obj is not Entity entity) return false;
    return Id == entity.Id;
}

public override int GetHashCode() => Id.GetHashCode();
}
```

This base class provides a standard structure for all entities, allowing them to be uniquely identified by their Id. By implementing equality methods, entities with the same Id are considered equal, helping to ensure consistency in comparisons.

Creating a Concrete Entity Let's implement a Customer entity, which represents a user in the system. The Customer entity will have properties like Name, Email, and Address, and methods to modify its state.

Example: Customer Entity

```
public class Customer : Entity
{
    public string Name { get; private set; }
    public string Email { get; private set; }
    public Address Address { get; private set; }

    public Customer(string name, string email, Address address)
    {
        Name = name;
        Email = email;
        Address = address;
    }

    public void UpdateEmail(string newEmail)
    {
        // Business rule to validate email format
        if (!IsValidEmail(newEmail)) throw new
        ArgumentException("Invalid email format.");
        Email = newEmail;
```

```
    }

    private bool IsValidEmail(string email) =>
        Regex.IsMatch(email, @"^[\w-\.]+@([\w-]+\.)+[\w-]{2,4}$");
}
```

In this example, the Customer entity has encapsulated fields and a method UpdateEmail that modifies the email address while enforcing a validation rule. By encapsulating the email update logic within the Customer entity, we ensure that the business rule for valid emails is consistently applied.

Implementing Value Objects

Value objects represent specific domain values without a unique identity. They are immutable, meaning that once created, they cannot be changed. C#9 records are ideal for implementing value objects, as they support immutability and equality based on property values.

Example: Address Value Object

```
public record Address(string Street, string City, string ZipCode);
```

With this record type, the Address value object is immutable. Two Address instances with the same values for Street, City, and ZipCode are considered equal, which is often desired behavior for value objects.

Using value objects within entities, such as assigning an Address to a Customer, ensures that specific data is treated consistently throughout the application.

Creating Aggregates

An aggregate is a cluster of entities and value objects with a defined root entity, known as the aggregate root. The aggregate root is responsible for maintaining the consistency of the aggregate, meaning all modifications to entities within the aggregate must go through the root.

Example: Order Aggregate

Let's create an Order aggregate with an aggregate root (Order) and an associated entity (OrderItem). The Order root will control modifications to its OrderItems, ensuring consistency.

Order and OrderItem Example

```
public class Order : Entity
{
    public DateTime OrderDate { get; private set; }
    public List<OrderItem> Items { get; private set; } = new
    List<OrderItem>();

    public Order(DateTime orderDate)
    {
        OrderDate = orderDate;
    }

    public void AddItem(Product product, int quantity)
    {
        var item = new OrderItem(product, quantity);
        Items.Add(item);
    }
}

public class OrderItem
{
    public Product Product { get; }
    public int Quantity { get; }

    public OrderItem(Product product, int quantity)
    {
        Product = product;
        Quantity = quantity;
    }
}
```

In this example, Order is the aggregate root. OrderItems can only be added to Order through the AddItem method in Order, maintaining consistency within the aggregate.

Implementing Domain Services

Domain services encapsulate business logic that doesn't naturally belong within a single entity. Domain services are typically stateless and operate on multiple entities or aggregates. Implement them in cases where functionality involves multiple entities or aggregates working together to complete a business rule.

Example: Order Processing Service

```
public class OrderProcessingService
{
    public decimal CalculateTotal(Order order)
    {
        return order.Items.Sum(item => item.Product.Price *
        item.Quantity);
    }

    public bool IsEligibleForDiscount(Order order)
    {
        return order.Items.Count >= 5;
    }
}
```

In this example, OrderProcessingService provides methods to calculate the total cost of an order and determine discount eligibility. These functions operate on the Order aggregate but don't belong directly within the Order entity, so we use a domain service to encapsulate them.

Leveraging Interfaces in the Core Layer

Clean architecture often involves defining interfaces in the core layer. Interfaces establish contracts that other layers, such as infrastructure or application, must implement. By defining interfaces in the core layer, we adhere to the dependency inversion principle, which reduces coupling and makes the core layer independent of implementation details.

Example: Repository Interface

```
public interface ICustomerRepository
{
    Customer GetById(int id);
    void Add(Customer customer);
    void Remove(Customer customer);
}
```

Here, the ICustomerRepository interface defines methods for retrieving, adding, and removing Customer entities. The actual implementation will be provided in the infrastructure layer, allowing the core layer to remain agnostic of data storage details.

Benefits of the Core Layer in Clean Architecture

The core layer provides several benefits that support the principles of clean architecture:

1. **Encapsulation of Business Logic**: By centralizing the business rules in the core layer, we ensure that logic governing the application's behavior is consistent and organized.
2. **Modularity and Testability**: The core layer is isolated from infrastructure and presentation dependencies, making it easy to test. Each component, from entities to services, can be tested independently without relying on external dependencies.
3. **Adherence to Domain-Driven Design**: The core layer's structure aligns with domain-driven design principles, allowing developers to focus on modeling the business domain accurately. Concepts like entities, value objects, and aggregates help create a rich and expressive model.
4. **Framework Independence**: By avoiding dependencies on frameworks or libraries, the core layer remains portable and adaptable to future changes in technology. This framework independence supports the clean architecture goal of minimal coupling with external systems.

31

The Application Layer: Coordinating the Flow

The application layer is the command center of clean architecture, orchestrating the flow of information between the core domain and the external world. While the domain layer defines the core business rules and entities, the application layer coordinates the various operations, or use cases, required by the business. It takes requests from the user interface, processes them according to the business rules, and then directs the necessary responses back to the user.

The purpose of the application layer is to coordinate and facilitate the execution of business use cases without directly handling business logic or technical implementations. In this chapter, we'll discuss how to structure the application layer, implement use cases, and apply patterns like Command Query Responsibility Segregation (CQRS) to streamline the application's functionality.

The Role of the Application Layer

The application layer acts as the middleman between the domain layer (core business logic) and the presentation layer (UI) or infrastructure layer (data storage, external services). Its responsibilities include:

1. **Orchestrating Use Cases**: The application layer defines and coordinates business use cases such as "Place Order," "Register User," or "Process Payment." Each use case encapsulates a specific business

operation.

2. **Managing Application Flow**: This layer directs the flow of information between the domain and infrastructure layers, ensuring the core rules are enforced while keeping the application flow consistent.

3. **Handling Transactions and Security**: The application layer can manage transactions, logging, and security checks, ensuring that the entire process is completed successfully or rolled back if an error occurs.

4. **Isolating the Domain Layer**: It separates the domain layer from direct access to infrastructure, allowing for independent testing and maintenance of business logic without external dependencies.

5. **Adapting to Presentation Needs**: It prepares the necessary data for the presentation layer, converting domain objects or results into specific data transfer objects (DTOs) that are easy to render or send in API responses.

Structuring the Application Layer

A well-structured application layer organizes code around use cases, making it easy to add, modify, or remove features without disrupting other parts of the application. Here's a recommended folder structure for the application layer:

- **UseCases**: A folder containing the core use cases of the application, each representing a business operation.
- **DTOs (Data Transfer Objects)**: Objects that structure data for communication between layers, especially between the application and presentation layers.
- **Interfaces**: Interfaces defining the structure for services or external dependencies, often implemented by the infrastructure layer.
- **Mediators or Handlers**: Mediators help facilitate communication between different parts of the application layer, often coordinating multiple use cases or queries.

Organizing the application layer in this way helps ensure a clear separation of concerns, with each use case or query clearly defined and isolated from others.

Implementing Use Cases

A use case is an application-level operation that coordinates specific business functions. In the application layer, each use case encapsulates one core function, making it easy to follow the single responsibility principle. For example, "PlaceOrder," "RegisterUser," or "ApplyDiscount" would each be separate use cases, each with a well-defined structure.

Example: Use Case for Placing an Order

Let's create a use case that coordinates the "Place Order" operation, involving the following steps:

1. Validate the order data.
2. Check inventory availability.
3. Calculate the total amount and any applicable discounts.
4. Save the order to the database.

PlaceOrderRequest DTO

```
public record PlaceOrderRequest(int CustomerId, List<OrderItemDTO>
Items);
```

OrderItemDTO

```
public record OrderItemDTO(int ProductId, int Quantity);
```

The PlaceOrderRequest DTO captures the details of the order being placed. Each item in the order is represented by the OrderItemDTO, which includes the product ID and quantity.

PlaceOrder Use Case

```
public class PlaceOrder
{
    private readonly IOrderRepository _orderRepository;
    private readonly IInventoryService _inventoryService;
    private readonly IDiscountService _discountService;

    public PlaceOrder(IOrderRepository orderRepository,
    IInventoryService inventoryService, IDiscountService
    discountService)
    {
        _orderRepository = orderRepository;
        _inventoryService = inventoryService;
        _discountService = discountService;
    }

    public async Task<int> ExecuteAsync(PlaceOrderRequest request)
    {
        // Validate order items
        foreach (var item in request.Items)
        {
            if
            (!_inventoryService.IsProductAvailable(item.ProductId,
            item.Quantity))
                throw new ArgumentException("Product not available
                in the requested quantity.");
        }

        // Calculate total with discounts
        var totalAmount =
        _discountService.ApplyDiscounts(request.Items);

        // Create and save order
        var order = new Order(request.CustomerId, DateTime.UtcNow,
        totalAmount);
        await _orderRepository.AddAsync(order);

        return order.Id;
    }
}
```

In this example, the PlaceOrder use case is responsible for coordinating

35

the business logic involved in placing an order. It verifies that products are available, applies discounts, and then creates an order entity to be stored in the database. By keeping this logic within the application layer, the core business rules (checking availability and applying discounts) remain encapsulated within the domain, while the orchestration is handled here.

Command Query Responsibility Segregation (CQRS)

CQRS is a design pattern that separates read (query) and write (command) operations. By isolating commands and queries, CQRS ensures that operations that modify data (commands) are handled separately from those that retrieve data (queries). In the application layer, CQRS provides a clear structure for implementing use cases and data access.

1. **Commands**: Commands represent actions that change the state of the application. Each command focuses on a specific operation, such as "create," "update," or "delete." They execute business rules, ensuring all state changes are properly validated and logged.
2. **Queries**: Queries retrieve data without altering application state. They may interact with a repository or a read-optimized database to get the information necessary for the user interface.

Example of a Query and a Command

Consider a scenario where we need to retrieve customer details (a query) and update customer information (a command).

GetCustomerDetails Query

```
public class GetCustomerDetails
{
    private readonly ICustomerRepository _customerRepository;

    public GetCustomerDetails(ICustomerRepository
    customerRepository)
    {
        _customerRepository = customerRepository;
```

```
    }

    public async Task<CustomerDTO> ExecuteAsync(int customerId)
    {
        var customer = await
        _customerRepository.GetByIdAsync(customerId);
        return new CustomerDTO(customer.Id, customer.Name,
        customer.Email);
    }
}
```

UpdateCustomerInfo Command

```
public class UpdateCustomerInfo
{
    private readonly ICustomerRepository _customerRepository;

    public UpdateCustomerInfo(ICustomerRepository
    customerRepository)
    {
        _customerRepository = customerRepository;
    }

    public async Task ExecuteAsync(int customerId, string newEmail)
    {
        var customer = await
        _customerRepository.GetByIdAsync(customerId);
        customer.UpdateEmail(newEmail);
        await _customerRepository.UpdateAsync(customer);
    }
}
```

With CQRS, the GetCustomerDetails query is solely responsible for retrieving customer data, while the UpdateCustomerInfo command is responsible for updating the customer's email. This separation simplifies the structure, making it easier to manage changes and validate operations independently.

Handling Data Transformation with DTOs

The application layer often needs to transform data between the domain layer and the presentation layer. Data Transfer Objects (DTOs) provide a solution by structuring data for specific application flows, such as returning JSON responses in an API. Unlike entities in the core domain, DTOs are lightweight and designed purely for transferring data, keeping business logic out of the data representation.

For instance, you might have a CustomerDTO for retrieving customer information:

CustomerDTO

```
public record CustomerDTO(int Id, string Name, string Email);
```

Using DTOs ensures that only necessary information is exposed to the user interface while keeping the internal structure of domain entities hidden.

Implementing Interfaces for Dependency Injection

The application layer relies on services and repositories to execute operations, but it doesn't implement these dependencies directly. Instead, interfaces are defined in the core or application layers, with actual implementations provided by the infrastructure layer. This setup enables dependency injection, promoting testability and flexibility.

For example, the IOrderRepository interface could be defined in the application layer and implemented by the infrastructure layer using a database like Entity Framework.

IOrderRepository Interface

```
public interface IOrderRepository
{
    Task<Order> GetByIdAsync(int orderId);
    Task AddAsync(Order order);
    Task UpdateAsync(Order order);
}
```

By defining this interface in the application layer, any implementation that conforms to the interface can be injected into the use cases, ensuring loose coupling and easier testing.

Benefits of the Application Layer in Clean Architecture

The application layer provides a centralized structure that orchestrates business use cases without embedding business rules or technical details, ensuring a clean, modular codebase. Here are some benefits:

1. **Maintainability**: Each use case is isolated and self-contained, making it easier to manage and modify individual operations.
2. **Testability**: The use of interfaces and dependency injection in the application layer promotes easy unit testing, as dependencies can be mocked during testing.
3. **Clear Separation of Concerns**: Commands and queries separate read and write operations, simplifying data flow and reducing complexity.
4. **Adaptability**: By transforming data between layers through DTOs, the application layer provides flexibility in handling changes to the data structure without impacting the core business logic.

The Infrastructure Layer: Implementing Persistence and External Integrations

T he infrastructure layer serves as the technical foundation of an application within clean architecture. It's responsible for managing data storage, external services, APIs, and any technical implementation required to fulfill the application's needs. Unlike the core or application layers, which are focused on business logic and coordination, the infrastructure layer handles the "plumbing" of the application, connecting it to databases, message queues, email servers, and more. This separation allows the infrastructure to support the application without cluttering core business logic with technical details.

In this chapter, we'll discuss the role of the infrastructure layer, how it implements persistence through repositories, how to set up external integrations, and best practices for keeping this layer independent and modular.

Purpose of the Infrastructure Layer

The infrastructure layer provides implementations for the interfaces defined in the core or application layers. Its main responsibilities include:

1. **Data Persistence**: Storing, retrieving, and updating data in databases, file systems, or cloud storage.
2. **External Integrations**: Connecting with external systems, such as APIs, messaging services, email services, or caching systems.

3. **Infrastructure Services**: Implementing cross-cutting services such as logging, authentication, and caching.
4. **Isolation of Technical Details**: Keeping the technical implementations separate from the business logic, allowing the application to focus solely on domain-specific operations.

Structuring the Infrastructure Layer

A well-organized infrastructure layer enhances maintainability and ensures that each component is easily accessible and modifiable. Below is a recommended folder structure:

- **Repositories**: Contains classes for data persistence, implementing repository interfaces defined in the core or application layers.
- **ExternalServices**: Houses services for integrating with external systems, like payment gateways or third-party APIs.
- **Persistence**: Includes database configuration files, migrations, and Entity Framework context classes.
- **Configurations**: Holds configuration settings for external services or databases, often sourced from appsettings.json or environment variables.

By separating each of these concerns within the infrastructure layer, you ensure modularity and promote a clean, organized architecture.

Implementing Repositories

Repositories are responsible for data access in the infrastructure layer, acting as intermediaries between the application's core logic and the database. Each repository class implements an interface defined in the core or application layer, ensuring that the infrastructure layer follows the dependency inversion principle.

Example of a Customer Repository

Let's say we have an ICustomerRepository interface defined in the application layer. The infrastructure layer will implement this interface in the CustomerRepository class, which uses Entity Framework Core to interact

41

with a SQL database.

ICustomerRepository Interface

```
public interface ICustomerRepository
{
    Task<Customer> GetByIdAsync(int id);
    Task<IEnumerable<Customer>> GetAllAsync();
    Task AddAsync(Customer customer);
    Task UpdateAsync(Customer customer);
    Task DeleteAsync(int id);
}
```

CustomerRepository Implementation

```
public class CustomerRepository : ICustomerRepository
{
    private readonly ApplicationDbContext _context;

    public CustomerRepository(ApplicationDbContext context)
    {
        _context = context;
    }

    public async Task<Customer> GetByIdAsync(int id)
    {
        return await _context.Customers.FindAsync(id);
    }

    public async Task<IEnumerable<Customer>> GetAllAsync()
    {
        return await _context.Customers.ToListAsync();
    }

    public async Task AddAsync(Customer customer)
    {
        await _context.Customers.AddAsync(customer);
        await _context.SaveChangesAsync();
    }
```

```
public async Task UpdateAsync(Customer customer)
{
    _context.Customers.Update(customer);
    await _context.SaveChangesAsync();
}

public async Task DeleteAsync(int id)
{
    var customer = await _context.Customers.FindAsync(id);
    if (customer != null)
    {
        _context.Customers.Remove(customer);
        await _context.SaveChangesAsync();
    }
}
}
```

In this example, the CustomerRepository class uses Entity Framework Core to implement the methods defined in the ICustomerRepository interface. Each method performs a specific data operation, such as retrieving, adding, or deleting a Customer record.

Configuring the Database Context with Entity Framework Core

The ApplicationDbContext class is an essential part of the infrastructure layer, responsible for managing database interactions. In a clean architecture application, the ApplicationDbContext is typically configured in the infrastructure layer, but it should be referenced from the application layer through dependency injection.

Example of ApplicationDbContext

```
public class ApplicationDbContext : DbContext
{
    public DbSet<Customer> Customers { get; set; }
    public DbSet<Order> Orders { get; set; }

    public ApplicationDbContext(DbContextOptions
```

```
<ApplicationDbContext> options)
        : base(options)
    {
    }

    protected override void OnModelCreating(ModelBuilder
    modelBuilder)
    {
        // Custom configurations go here
        modelBuilder.Entity<Customer>().HasIndex(c =>
        c.Email).IsUnique();
    }
}
```

In this ApplicationDbContext, we define DbSet properties for Customer and Order entities, which represent tables in the database. The OnModelCreating method allows us to customize table structures and relationships, such as enforcing unique constraints.

Database Configuration in appsettings.json

```
{
    "ConnectionStrings": {
        "DefaultConnection": "Server=.;
Database=CleanArchitectureDb;
Trusted_Connection=True;"
    }
}
```

Configuring Dependency Injection for the DbContext

```
services.AddDbContext<
ApplicationDbContext>(options =>
    options.UseSqlServer(Configuration.
GetConnectionString("DefaultConnection")));
```

Adding the database context to dependency injection in the Startup.cs or Program.cs file ensures it can be injected into repository classes within the infrastructure layer, making database access convenient and modular.

Integrating External Services

The infrastructure layer is also responsible for integrating with external services, such as payment gateways, email providers, or third-party APIs. Each external service should have its interface defined in the application layer, with the actual implementation residing in the infrastructure layer.

Example: Email Service Integration

Suppose we want to send emails using a third-party provider like SendGrid. We'd start by defining an IEmailService interface in the application layer:

IEmailService Interface

```
public interface IEmailService
{
    Task SendEmailAsync(string to,
 string subject, string body);
}
```

Then, implement this interface in the infrastructure layer, using SendGrid's API:

SendGridEmailService Implementation

```
public class SendGridEmailService : IEmailService
{
    private readonly SendGridClient _client;
    private readonly string _fromEmail;

    public SendGridEmailService
(string apiKey, string fromEmail)
    {
        _client = new SendGridClient(apiKey);
        _fromEmail = fromEmail;
    }

    public async Task SendEmailAsync
(string to, string subject, string body)
```

```
    {
        var msg = new SendGridMessage()
        {
            From = new EmailAddress(_fromEmail),
            Subject = subject,
            HtmlContent = body
        };
        msg.AddTo(new EmailAddress(to));
        await _client.SendEmailAsync(msg);
    }
}
```

By injecting the SendGridEmailService wherever the IEmailService interface is used, you keep email functionality flexible and independent of specific implementation details.

Using Dependency Injection for Flexibility

Dependency injection is crucial in the infrastructure layer, as it promotes flexibility and makes testing easier. By injecting services, repositories, and configurations, we keep dependencies loosely coupled, making it easy to swap out implementations as needed.

For example, in the Startup.cs or Program.cs file, you might configure dependency injection as follows:

```
services.AddScoped<ICustomerRepository,
  CustomerRepository>();
services.AddTransient<IEmailService,
  SendGridEmailService>();
```

By injecting dependencies like this, you allow the application to remain agnostic of the underlying implementations, improving maintainability and testability.

Best Practices for the Infrastructure Layer

To keep the infrastructure layer effective and maintainable, follow these best practices:

1. **Use Interfaces for Dependency Management**: Always define inter-faces for infrastructure dependencies in the core or application layers. Implement these interfaces in the infrastructure layer, allowing for clear separation and loose coupling.

2. **Separate Configuration from Code**: Store configuration settings for databases and external services in appsettings.json or environment variables. Avoid hard-coding configuration details directly in the classes to keep them flexible and secure.

3. **Handle Exceptions Gracefully**: Implement error handling and logging for all external services. When working with APIs or databases, ensure that exceptions are caught and managed gracefully, logging any necessary information for troubleshooting.

4. **Limit Cross-Layer References**: The infrastructure layer should depend on the application and core layers but not the other way around. This one-way dependency flow maintains the clean architecture principle of dependency inversion.

5. **Make External Services Easily Replaceable**: For third-party services like payment providers or email gateways, create flexible implementations so they can be replaced without major code changes. Dependency injection makes this approach straightforward.

Testing the Infrastructure Layer

Testing in the infrastructure layer is often focused on integration tests, as it directly interacts with external systems. Consider creating separate testing projects for integration tests that validate the infrastructure's functionality, such as database operations or API integrations.

For instance, to test CustomerRepository, you can use an in-memory database like SQLite for integration testing:

```
public class CustomerRepositoryTests
{
    private readonly CustomerRepository _repository;
    private readonly ApplicationDbContext _context;
```

```
    public CustomerRepositoryTests()
    {
        var options = new
        DbContextOptionsBuilder<ApplicationDbContext>()
            .UseInMemoryDatabase
 (databaseName: "TestDatabase")
            .Options;
        _context = new ApplicationDbContext(options);
        _repository = new CustomerRepository(_context);
    }

    // Test methods go here, e.g.,
  AddAsync, GetByIdAsync, etc.
 }
```

Using in-memory databases or mock services enables you to simulate external dependencies, ensuring that the infrastructure layer behaves as expected without needing actual external resources.

Building the Presentation Layer with ASP.NET Core

T he presentation layer, often referred to as the interface layer, is responsible for handling user interactions, processing input, and delivering output. In a web application, this layer includes APIs, controllers, views, and UI elements that enable users to interact with the underlying business logic. In clean architecture, the presentation layer is designed to stay focused on user interactions, maintaining a clear separation from the core domain and application layers.

In this chapter, we'll explore how to build an effective presentation layer using ASP.NET Core. We'll cover setting up API controllers, structuring MVC (Model-View-Controller) components, transforming data with ViewModels, and handling user requests in a way that keeps the architecture clean and maintainable.

The Role of the Presentation Layer

The presentation layer serves as the entry point to the application, responsible for:

1. **Accepting and Validating Input**: Handling user requests and validating inputs before passing them to the application layer.
2. **Routing and Controller Logic**: Directing user requests to the appropriate use cases or application services.
3. **Managing View Models and Responses**: Formatting data and re-

sponses into a suitable structure for the user interface, whether in JSON or HTML.

4. **Maintaining Separation of Concerns**: Ensuring that the UI layer focuses solely on presentation tasks, leaving business logic to the application and domain layers.

The presentation layer interacts with the application layer only through use cases, service interfaces, or application layer DTOs, avoiding any direct dependency on the core domain or infrastructure layers.

Structuring the Presentation Layer

In an ASP.NET Core application, the presentation layer is structured around MVC components, making it easy to manage API controllers, views, and models. Below is a recommended folder structure:

- **Controllers**: Handles incoming HTTP requests and routes them to the appropriate application logic.
- **ViewModels**: Contains classes that structure data for the user interface, tailored to the needs of specific views or API responses.
- **Filters**: Defines reusable components for handling cross-cutting concerns like authorization, logging, and error handling.

With this structure, each component has a specific role, contributing to a clean and manageable codebase.

Setting Up API Controllers

In a clean architecture application, controllers act as the entry points to specific use cases or operations, routing user requests to the appropriate services. ASP.NET Core's API controllers are ideal for building RESTful APIs that interact with the application layer.

Example: CustomerController

Let's create a CustomerController that manages customer-related operations such as adding, updating, and retrieving customer information. This controller interacts with the application layer to process requests and deliver responses in JSON format.

```
[ApiController]
[Route("api/[controller]")]
public class CustomerController : ControllerBase
{
    private readonly ICustomerService _customerService;

    public CustomerController(ICustomerService customerService)
    {
        _customerService = customerService;
    }

    [HttpGet("{id}")]
    public async Task<IActionResult> GetCustomer(int id)
    {
        var customer = await
        _customerService.GetCustomerByIdAsync(id);
        if (customer == null)
            return NotFound();

        return Ok(customer);
    }

    [HttpPost]
    public async Task<IActionResult>
    CreateCustomer(CreateCustomerRequest request)
    {
        var customerId = await
        _customerService.CreateCustomerAsync(request);
        return CreatedAtAction(nameof(GetCustomer), new { id =
        customerId }, customerId);
    }

    [HttpPut("{id}")]
    public async Task<IActionResult> UpdateCustomer(int id,
    UpdateCustomerRequest request)
    {
        var success = await
```

```
        _customerService.UpdateCustomerAsync(id, request);
        if (!success)
            return NotFound();

        return NoContent();
    }
}
```

In this example, the CustomerController has actions for retrieving, creating, and updating customer records. Each action method calls a service method in the application layer, ensuring that the controller itself remains focused on managing HTTP requests rather than performing business logic.

Validating Input with Data Annotations

Input validation is critical for ensuring data integrity and preventing errors from propagating through the application. ASP.NET Core provides data annotations that allow you to add validation directly to DTOs or ViewModels, ensuring that inputs meet specified criteria before they reach the application layer.

Example: CreateCustomerRequest DTO with Validation

```
public class CreateCustomerRequest
{
    [Required]
    [StringLength(50)]
    public string Name { get; set; }

    [Required]
    [EmailAddress]
    public string Email { get; set; }

    [Required]
    [StringLength(100)]
    public string Address { get; set; }
}
```

By adding data annotations like [Required] and [StringLength], the CreateCus tomerRequest DTO enforces validation rules. ASP.NET Core automatically checks these rules when the request is received, returning a 400 Bad Request response if validation fails.

Mapping Data with ViewModels

ViewModels are designed to structure data for the presentation layer, transforming it into formats that are easy to display or transmit. While entities in the core layer focus on business logic, ViewModels are solely concerned with data display, ensuring that the user interface remains separate from the domain.

Example: CustomerViewModel

```
public class CustomerViewModel
{
    public int Id { get; set; }
    public string Name { get; set; }
    public string Email { get; set; }
}
```

Mapping Example in CustomerService In the application layer, you can map entities or DTOs to ViewModels before returning data to the presentation layer.

```
public async Task<CustomerViewModel> GetCustomerByIdAsync(int id)
{
    var customer = await _customerRepository.GetByIdAsync(id);
    return new CustomerViewModel
    {
        Id = customer.Id,
        Name = customer.Name,
        Email = customer.Email
    };
}
```

Using ViewModels helps keep the presentation layer independent of domain entities and core business rules, supporting a clean and decoupled architecture.

Handling Cross-Cutting Concerns with Filters

Filters are a powerful feature in ASP.NET Core that allow you to encapsulate cross-cutting concerns like logging, authentication, and error handling. By defining custom filters, you can keep controllers focused on request handling, while reusable logic like logging or authentication is managed separately.

Example: Custom Logging Filter

```
public class LoggingFilter : IActionFilter
{
    private readonly ILogger<LoggingFilter> _logger;

    public LoggingFilter(ILogger<LoggingFilter> logger)
    {
        _logger = logger;
    }

    public void OnActionExecuting(ActionExecutingContext context)
    {
        _logger.LogInformation("Executing action {ActionName}",
        context.ActionDescriptor.DisplayName);
    }

    public void OnActionExecuted(ActionExecutedContext context)
    {
        _logger.LogInformation("Executed action {ActionName}",
        context.ActionDescriptor.DisplayName);
    }
}
```

You can register the filter globally or apply it selectively to specific controllers or actions, depending on your needs. This approach keeps your controllers clean while ensuring essential functionality is applied consistently.

Error Handling and Exception Filters

To manage errors effectively, the presentation layer can use exception filters to catch and handle unhandled exceptions gracefully. ASP.NET Core provides a default exception filter, but custom filters can be implemented to customize the error-handling experience.

Example: Custom Exception Filter

```
public class CustomExceptionFilter : IExceptionFilter
{
    private readonly ILogger<CustomExceptionFilter> _logger;

    public CustomExceptionFilter(ILogger<CustomExceptionFilter>
    logger)
    {
        _logger = logger;
    }

    public void OnException(ExceptionContext context)
    {
        _logger.LogError(context.Exception, "An unhandled
        exception occurred.");
        context.Result = new ObjectResult("An error occurred while
        processing your request.")
        {
            StatusCode = StatusCodes.Status500InternalServerError
        };
    }
}
```

Using a custom exception filter like this one allows you to log errors and return user-friendly messages to the client, enhancing the user experience.

Best Practices for the Presentation Layer

To maintain a clean and effective presentation layer, follow these best practices:

1. **Avoid Business Logic in Controllers**: Keep controllers focused on managing HTTP requests and responses. All business logic should reside

in the application or domain layers.

2. **Use Dependency Injection**: Inject dependencies like services and repositories into controllers rather than creating instances within the controller. This approach promotes testability and maintainability.

3. **Handle Validation and Error Management Gracefully**: Use data annotations for input validation, and implement custom filters for consistent error handling. This keeps the code clean and the user experience smooth.

4. **Separate Data Display Logic**: Use ViewModels to structure data specifically for the user interface, avoiding direct use of domain entities in API responses. This approach supports separation of concerns and minimizes data leakage.

5. **Keep Routing Consistent**: Ensure that API routes are consistent and follow RESTful principles. Use route conventions to make it easy for developers to understand and work with your API.

Testing the Presentation Layer

Testing the presentation layer involves verifying that the controllers return expected responses and handle different scenarios appropriately. Unit tests can be created for individual controller methods, often using mock dependencies for services. ASP.NET Core also supports integration testing, allowing you to verify that the application works as expected end-to-end.

Example: Unit Test for CustomerController

```
public class CustomerControllerTests
{
    private readonly Mock<ICustomerService> _mockService;
    private readonly CustomerController _controller;

    public CustomerControllerTests()
    {
        _mockService = new Mock<ICustomerService>();
        _controller = new CustomerController(_mockService.Object);
    }
}
```

```
[Fact]
public async Task
GetCustomer_ReturnsOkResult_WhenCustomerExists()
{
    // Arrange
    var customer = new CustomerViewModel { Id = 1, Name =
    "John Doe", Email = "john@example.com" };
    _mockService.Setup(service =>
    service.GetCustomerByIdAsync(1)).ReturnsAsync(customer);

    // Act
    var result = await _controller.GetCustomer(1);

    // Assert
    var okResult = Assert.IsType<OkObjectResult>(result);
    Assert.Equal(customer, okResult.Value);
}
}
```

In this example, the test verifies that GetCustomer returns an OkObjectResult when the customer exists. By mocking ICustomerService, we isolate the controller's behavior, allowing us to focus solely on presentation logic.

Testing and Test-Driven Development (TDD)

T esting is a critical component of software development, ensuring that an application functions as intended and maintains reliability over time. In clean architecture, testing is especially important because each layer operates independently, requiring robust tests to verify the behavior of individual components. Test-driven development (TDD) takes testing a step further by incorporating testing into the development process itself. TDD promotes building applications by writing tests before the actual code, leading to cleaner, more maintainable code and reducing the risk of bugs and regressions.

In this chapter, we'll explore testing fundamentals, how TDD fits into clean architecture, and how to implement effective tests for each layer. We'll cover unit testing, integration testing, and best practices for using TDD to achieve reliable, high-quality software.

Understanding the Role of Testing in Clean Architecture

Testing is essential for clean architecture, where a modular structure with well-defined boundaries supports scalability, maintainability, and independence between components. Each layer—the core, application, infrastructure, and presentation—requires specific testing strategies to ensure it operates independently and correctly within the overall system.

1. **Unit Tests**: Unit tests focus on individual components, ensuring they

work as expected in isolation. They validate the smallest testable parts, such as a single function, class, or method, without external dependencies.

2. **Integration Tests**: Integration tests examine how different layers or components work together, verifying the interaction between modules, such as the application layer's interaction with the infrastructure layer.

3. **End-to-End Tests**: These tests simulate real user behavior, validating the entire system flow from start to finish, ensuring that the application performs as expected across all layers and dependencies.

The Principles of Test-Driven Development (TDD)

Test-driven development is a development methodology that integrates testing into the development process itself. TDD operates on three main steps, often summarized as **Red-Green-Refactor**:

1. **Red**: Write a failing test for a specific feature or behavior before writing the actual code.

2. **Green**: Write the simplest code necessary to make the test pass.

3. **Refactor**: Clean up the code, optimizing and improving it while ensuring that all tests still pass.

This approach emphasizes building software in small, testable increments, leading to more reliable and maintainable code. By following TDD, developers can also ensure that the application's requirements are well-defined and validated from the start.

Implementing Unit Tests

Unit tests validate individual components or classes in isolation, providing immediate feedback on whether a specific function behaves as expected. In clean architecture, unit tests are especially useful for the core and application layers, where the business logic and use cases reside.

Example: Unit Test for a Domain Service

Let's consider a domain service in the core layer, DiscountService, that calculates discounts based on customer loyalty:

DiscountService Implementation

```
public class DiscountService
{
    public decimal CalculateDiscount(Customer customer)
    {
        if (customer.YearsWithCompany >= 5)
            return 0.20m;
        if (customer.YearsWithCompany >= 3)
            return 0.10m;

        return 0.0m;
    }
}
```

To test DiscountService, we create a unit test that verifies the discount calculation logic:

DiscountServiceTests

```
public class DiscountServiceTests
{
    private readonly DiscountService _discountService;

    public DiscountServiceTests()
    {
        _discountService = new DiscountService();
    }

    [Fact]
    public void
    CalculateDiscount_Returns20Percent_ForFiveYearsOrMore()
    {
        // Arrange
        var customer = new Customer { YearsWithCompany = 5 };

        // Act
        var discount =
```

```
    _discountService.CalculateDiscount(customer);

    // Assert
    Assert.Equal(0.20m, discount);
}

[Fact]
public void
CalculateDiscount_Returns10Percent_ForThreeYearsOrMore()
{
    var customer = new Customer { YearsWithCompany = 3 };
    var discount =
    _discountService.CalculateDiscount(customer);
    Assert.Equal(0.10m, discount);
}

[Fact]
public void
CalculateDiscount_ReturnsZero_ForLessThanThreeYears()
{
    var customer = new Customer { YearsWithCompany = 1 };
    var discount =
    _discountService.CalculateDiscount(customer);
    Assert.Equal(0.0m, discount);
}
}
```

In this test class, we verify that CalculateDiscount returns the correct discount percentage based on the customer's years with the company. Each test case focuses on a specific scenario, providing comprehensive coverage of the service's behavior.

Implementing TDD in the Application Layer

The application layer is responsible for orchestrating use cases, and TDD can help ensure that each use case behaves as expected. Testing the application layer typically involves mocking dependencies to isolate the functionality under test.

Example: TDD for a PlaceOrder Use Case

61

Let's create a simple test for a PlaceOrder use case that involves verifying product availability and calculating the total price before placing an order.

First Step: Write a Failing Test (Red)

```csharp
public class PlaceOrderTests
{
    private readonly Mock<IInventoryService> _mockInventoryService;
    private readonly Mock<IOrderRepository> _mockOrderRepository;
    private readonly PlaceOrder _placeOrder;

    public PlaceOrderTests()
    {
        _mockInventoryService = new Mock<IInventoryService>();
        _mockOrderRepository = new Mock<IOrderRepository>();
        _placeOrder = new PlaceOrder(_mockOrderRepository.Object,
        _mockInventoryService.Object);
    }

    [Fact]
    public async Task
    ExecuteAsync_ThrowsException_WhenProductIsUnavailable()
    {
        // Arrange
        var request = new PlaceOrderRequest(1, new
        List<OrderItemDTO> { new OrderItemDTO(1, 5) });
        _mockInventoryService.Setup(s =>
        s.IsProductAvailable(It.IsAny<int>(), It.IsAny<int>()))
            .Returns(false);

        // Act & Assert
        await Assert.ThrowsAsync<InvalidOperationException>(() =>
        _placeOrder.ExecuteAsync(request));
    }
}
```

Second Step: Implement Code to Pass the Test (Green)

```csharp
public class PlaceOrder
{
    private readonly IOrderRepository _orderRepository;
    private readonly IInventoryService _inventoryService;

    public PlaceOrder(IOrderRepository orderRepository,
    IInventoryService inventoryService)
    {
        _orderRepository = orderRepository;
        _inventoryService = inventoryService;
    }

    public async Task ExecuteAsync(PlaceOrderRequest request)
    {
        foreach (var item in request.Items)
        {
            if
            (!_inventoryService.IsProductAvailable(item.ProductId,
            item.Quantity))
                throw new InvalidOperationException("Product not
                available.");
        }

        // Additional logic for order placement goes here.
    }
}
```

After implementing the logic to pass the test, you can continue by writing additional tests for other aspects of the PlaceOrder use case, such as calculating the total price and saving the order.

Integration Testing with External Dependencies

Integration tests validate interactions between multiple components or layers. In clean architecture, integration tests commonly verify the behavior of the application and infrastructure layers, ensuring that repositories, APIs, and services function as expected.

For instance, to test a CustomerRepository that connects to a database, you can use an in-memory database to verify repository operations without

63

relying on a production database.

Example: Integration Test for CustomerRepository

```csharp
public class CustomerRepositoryTests
{
    private readonly CustomerRepository _repository;
    private readonly ApplicationDbContext _context;

    public CustomerRepositoryTests()
    {
        var options = new
        DbContextOptionsBuilder<ApplicationDbContext>()
            .UseInMemoryDatabase(databaseName: "TestDatabase")
            .Options;
        _context = new ApplicationDbContext(options);
        _repository = new CustomerRepository(_context);
    }

    [Fact]
    public async Task AddAsync_ShouldAddCustomerToDatabase()
    {
        var customer = new Customer { Name = "John Doe", Email =
        "john@example.com" };
        await _repository.AddAsync(customer);

        var retrievedCustomer = await
        _repository.GetByIdAsync(customer.Id);
        Assert.NotNull(retrievedCustomer);
        Assert.Equal("John Doe", retrievedCustomer.Name);
    }
}
```

This test verifies that AddAsync correctly adds a customer to the database by retrieving and asserting that the customer data matches the original input.

Mocking Dependencies and Isolation in Tests

To keep tests focused and independent, especially in the application layer, dependencies should be mocked. Mocking enables you to isolate a function or method without relying on its dependencies, allowing you to verify that it performs correctly under specific scenarios.

Example: Mocking Dependencies in Unit Tests

```
var mockCustomerRepository = new Mock<ICustomerRepository>();
mockCustomerRepository.Setup(repo =>
repo.GetByIdAsync(It.IsAny<int>()))
    .ReturnsAsync(new Customer { Id = 1, Name = "Jane Doe", Email
    = "jane@example.com" });
```

By setting up the mock repository, you can simulate specific scenarios without relying on actual implementations, making the test environment controlled and predictable.

Best Practices for Testing in Clean Architecture

To get the most out of your tests, follow these best practices for clean architecture:

1. **Test Behavior, Not Implementation**: Focus on testing how each layer behaves rather than testing specific code implementations, which allows for flexibility and adaptability as the code evolves.
2. **Use Mocking Libraries**: Use mocking libraries like Moq to isolate dependencies and test individual components independently. Mocking also simplifies the setup and allows you to focus on testing core functionality.
3. **Maintain Test Independence**: Ensure that each test case is independent, meaning it doesn't rely on other tests' data or outcomes. This approach keeps tests reliable and avoids cascading failures.
4. **Write Clear and Descriptive Tests**: Tests should be self-explanatory, with descriptive names and clear assertions that make it easy to understand what behavior is being validated.
5. **Automate Tests in CI/CD**: Integrate tests into your continuous integration/continuous deployment (CI/CD) pipeline. Automated tests ensure that code changes don't introduce regressions, providing consistent feedback during development.

Security in Clean Architecture Applications

S ecurity is a fundamental aspect of any application, ensuring that data remains protected and that unauthorized access is prevented. In a clean architecture application, security can be challenging because of the separation of layers and the need to keep each layer independent and focused on its specific responsibilities. However, by following security best practices and implementing specific safeguards in each layer, we can create a robust, secure application that upholds the principles of clean architecture.

In this chapter, we'll explore security considerations across the core, application, infrastructure, and presentation layers, covering topics like authentication, authorization, data protection, input validation, and secure configuration. By addressing security at each layer, we build a secure, well-structured application that mitigates risks and protects data.

Principles of Security in Clean Architecture

Security in clean architecture adheres to a few core principles:

1. **Defense in Depth**: Security should be implemented at multiple layers, with each layer protecting the next. If one layer is compromised, additional layers still provide protection.
2. **Least Privilege**: Limit access rights for users and components to the minimum necessary to perform their function. This principle applies both to user permissions and to interactions between layers.

3. **Separation of Concerns**: Each layer in clean architecture has a distinct purpose, and security implementations should not bleed into areas where they don't belong. For example, authentication and authorization should be handled in the presentation layer or the application layer, while encryption and data protection might be managed in the infrastructure layer.

4. **Zero Trust**: Never trust incoming data or requests, even if they originate from within the application. Always validate and sanitize inputs to prevent security vulnerabilities.

Security in the Core Layer

The core layer contains business entities, rules, and policies, making it an essential part of the application's functionality. Although security implementations are usually handled in other layers, the core layer can define specific security-related rules or validations as part of its business logic.

1. **Business Rules for Sensitive Data**: Define rules around sensitive data within entities. For example, a financial application might set rules that restrict access to financial transactions based on specific roles.

2. **Secure Domain Services**: In cases where certain operations require elevated permissions, ensure that domain services enforce these rules internally. For instance, a TransferService might verify user permissions before authorizing a transaction.

3. **Avoid Hard-Coding Sensitive Information**: Sensitive information, such as encryption keys or authentication tokens, should never be stored in the core layer. Use environment variables or configuration management tools to handle sensitive data in a secure way.

Security in the Application Layer

The application layer manages use cases and orchestrates the flow between the core and presentation layers. It's where user authentication and authorization checks are performed to ensure that requests adhere to security policies before they reach the core layer.

- **Authorization Policies**: Define role-based or claims-based authorization policies that check if a user is allowed to perform a specific action. Implement these checks as part of the application layer's use cases, which interact with the core logic.

Example: Authorization in Use Case

```
public class PlaceOrder
{
    private readonly IOrderRepository _orderRepository;
    private readonly IUserContext _userContext;

    public PlaceOrder(IOrderRepository orderRepository,
    IUserContext userContext)
    {
        _orderRepository = orderRepository;
        _userContext = userContext;
    }

    public async Task ExecuteAsync(OrderRequest request)
    {
        if (!_userContext.User.HasPermission("PLACE_ORDER"))
            throw new UnauthorizedAccessException("User does not
            have permission to place an order.");

        // Proceed with order placement...
    }
}
```

In this example, the PlaceOrder use case verifies if the user has the "PLACE_ORDER" permission before proceeding.

- **Input Validation**: Ensure that all inputs are validated to prevent injection attacks and other malicious activities. Validation should occur in the application layer before passing data to the core layer to ensure that invalid or malicious data is stopped early.
- **Secure Communication Between Layers**: Although the application

layer interacts primarily with the presentation and infrastructure layers, ensure that sensitive information is never exposed unnecessarily between layers. If sensitive data must be shared, use encryption or hashing to protect it.

Security in the Infrastructure Layer

The infrastructure layer handles data persistence, external service integrations, and other technical implementations. Security in this layer focuses on protecting stored data, securing external communications, and managing configuration settings.

- **Data Encryption and Hashing**: Encrypt sensitive data before storing it in a database. Use hashing algorithms for passwords and other sensitive information that doesn't need to be decrypted, ensuring one-way encryption.

Example: Hashing a Password with ASP.NET Core Identity

```
public class PasswordHasher
{
    private readonly IPasswordHasher<User> _passwordHasher;

    public PasswordHasher(IPasswordHasher<User> passwordHasher)
    {
        _passwordHasher = passwordHasher;
    }

    public string HashPassword(string password)
    {
        var user = new User(); // Placeholder user object for
        hashing
        return _passwordHasher.HashPassword(user, password);
    }
}
```

In this example, ASP.NET Core's IPasswordHasher is used to hash a password securely, making it safe for storage.

- **Secure External Integrations**: When integrating with external APIs or services, use secure communication protocols like HTTPS. Ensure that API keys, tokens, or secrets are stored securely in environment variables or secret management tools rather than in the codebase.
- **Configuration Management**: Store configuration settings, including connection strings, API keys, and tokens, securely in appsettings.json, environment variables, or a dedicated configuration management service. Avoid hard-coding sensitive information in the application code.
- **Database Security**: Use least-privilege principles for database access. Define different roles for reading and writing data and avoid giving the application excessive permissions. Regularly review database security settings, implement access controls, and audit database usage.
- **Logging and Monitoring**: Implement logging for critical actions, such as database access, file operations, and external service calls, to help detect suspicious activity. Ensure logs do not contain sensitive information like passwords or tokens, and securely store logs for auditing and monitoring purposes.

Security in the Presentation Layer

The presentation layer, which interacts directly with users, is often the first line of defense. This layer manages authentication, handles user requests, and presents data in a secure format.

- **Authentication**: Use secure authentication mechanisms, such as OAuth2, OpenID Connect, or JSON Web Tokens (JWT), to verify user identity. In ASP.NET Core, you can configure authentication schemes to protect your application against unauthorized access.

Example: JWT Authentication Setup

```
services.AddAuthentication(options =>
{
    options.DefaultAuthenticateScheme =
    JwtBearerDefaults.AuthenticationScheme;
    options.DefaultChallengeScheme =
    JwtBearerDefaults.AuthenticationScheme;
})
.AddJwtBearer(options =>
{
    options.TokenValidationParameters = new
    TokenValidationParameters
    {
        ValidateIssuer = true,
        ValidateAudience = true,
        ValidateLifetime = true,
        ValidateIssuerSigningKey = true,
        // Set issuer, audience, and signing key
    };
});
```

With JWT, you can ensure that only authenticated users have access to your application's resources, with token-based authentication providing stateless and secure access control.

- **Role-Based Access Control (RBAC)**: Implement role-based access to limit what each user role can access or modify. For instance, only admins should have permission to delete users or modify sensitive data.

Example: Role-Based Authorization in ASP.NET Core

```
[Authorize(Roles = "Admin")]
public class AdminController : ControllerBase
{
    // Admin-only actions
}
```

- **Cross-Site Request Forgery (CSRF) Protection**: CSRF attacks trick users into performing unwanted actions on a web application in which they are authenticated. ASP.NET Core provides built-in CSRF protection through anti-forgery tokens that verify the source of requests.

Example: Enabling CSRF in ASP.NET Core

```
services.AddControllersWithViews(options =>
{
    options.Filters.Add(new
    AutoValidateAntiforgeryTokenAttribute());
});
```

- **Input Validation and Output Encoding**: Protect against injection attacks (SQL, XSS) by validating all inputs and encoding outputs. For instance, sanitize HTML inputs to prevent XSS vulnerabilities and use parameterized queries or ORM tools to avoid SQL injection.
- **Error Handling and Exception Management**: Avoid revealing sensitive information through error messages. Use custom error handling to log exceptions securely and provide generic error responses to users without exposing implementation details.

Example: Custom Exception Middleware in ASP.NET Core

```
public class CustomExceptionMiddleware
{
    private readonly RequestDelegate _next;
    private readonly ILogger<CustomExceptionMiddleware> _logger;

    public CustomExceptionMiddleware(RequestDelegate next,
    ILogger<CustomExceptionMiddleware> logger)
    {
        _next = next;
        _logger = logger;
```

```
    }

    public async Task InvokeAsync(HttpContext context)
    {
        try
        {
            await _next(context);
        }
        catch (Exception ex)
        {
            _logger.LogError(ex, "An error occurred.");
            context.Response.StatusCode =
            StatusCodes.Status500InternalServerError;
            await context.Response.WriteAsync("An unexpected error
            occurred.");
        }
    }
}
```

This middleware captures unhandled exceptions, logs them securely, and returns a generic error message to the client.

Best Practices for Security in Clean Architecture

To create a secure application within a clean architecture framework, follow these best practices:

1. **Use Dependency Injection for Security Services**: Inject authentication, authorization, and encryption services through dependency injection to simplify testing and management.
2. **Regularly Review and Update Security Configurations**: Regularly review configurations, including access policies, connection strings, and tokens. Update as needed to comply with best practices and security standards.
3. **Audit and Monitor Security Logs**: Implement logging for security-critical actions and regularly review logs to detect and address suspicious activities.

4. **Implement Secure Coding Practices**: Avoid common vulnerabilities by following secure coding practices, such as input validation, output encoding, and parameterized queries.

5. **Encrypt Sensitive Data**: Encrypt sensitive data at rest and in transit. Use HTTPS for web applications, and encrypt any sensitive information stored in databases or logs.

Applying Asynchronous Programming with C#9 and .NET 5

I n today's fast-paced, data-driven applications, responsiveness and scalability are crucial. Asynchronous programming enables developers to handle tasks without blocking threads, improving application performance and responsiveness, especially in I/O-bound operations like database calls, file access, and network requests. With C#9 and .NET 5, asynchronous programming has evolved, offering new language features and performance improvements that align well with clean architecture principles.

In this chapter, we'll explore how asynchronous programming works in C#9 and .NET 5, the benefits it brings to clean architecture, and how to apply it effectively in each layer of the application. We'll also cover best practices for handling asynchronous tasks, avoiding common pitfalls, and testing asynchronous code.

Understanding Asynchronous Programming in .NET 5

Asynchronous programming in .NET is primarily enabled by the async and await keywords, which simplify writing asynchronous code. The primary goal of asynchronous programming is to prevent threads from blocking while waiting for an I/O operation to complete, freeing up resources to handle other tasks concurrently.

1. **Async and Await**: async and await allow methods to be defined as asynchronous, where await releases the calling thread to perform other

work while waiting for the task to complete.

2. **Task and Task<T>**: Tasks represent asynchronous operations that may produce a result (Task<T>) or complete without a result (Task). These are the core types used for managing asynchronous operations in .NET.

3. **ValueTask and IAsyncEnumerable**: Newer additions like ValueTask and IAsyncEnumerable in C#9 offer efficient alternatives for high-performance, low-overhead asynchronous programming.

By leveraging these tools, asynchronous programming can be applied across the layers of clean architecture, allowing each layer to perform efficiently without blocking resources.

Benefits of Asynchronous Programming in Clean Architecture

In a clean architecture application, each layer has specific tasks that can benefit from asynchronous programming:

1. **Improved Responsiveness**: By executing I/O operations asynchronously, the application remains responsive, even when handling multiple requests or processing large datasets.

2. **Better Resource Utilization**: Asynchronous programming releases threads to handle other tasks, optimizing the use of system resources and increasing scalability.

3. **Enhanced User Experience**: For user-facing applications, asynchronous programming improves responsiveness and load times, enhancing the overall user experience.

4. **Scalability in Web Applications**: In web applications, asynchronous controllers and services enable efficient request handling, allowing the application to scale under high load without compromising performance.

Applying Asynchronous Programming in the Infrastructure Layer

The infrastructure layer often performs data access and external integrations, which are typically I/O-bound operations that benefit significantly from asynchronous programming.

Example: Asynchronous Repository Implementation

Let's implement a CustomerRepository with asynchronous methods for accessing a database. Using Entity Framework Core, we can perform operations like retrieving or saving data without blocking threads.

```csharp
public class CustomerRepository : ICustomerRepository
{
    private readonly ApplicationDbContext _context;

    public CustomerRepository(ApplicationDbContext context)
    {
        _context = context;
    }

    public async Task<Customer> GetByIdAsync(int id)
    {
        return await _context.Customers.FindAsync(id);
    }

    public async Task<IEnumerable<Customer>> GetAllAsync()
    {
        return await _context.Customers.ToListAsync();
    }

    public async Task AddAsync(Customer customer)
    {
        await _context.Customers.AddAsync(customer);
        await _context.SaveChangesAsync();
    }

    public async Task UpdateAsync(Customer customer)
    {
        _context.Customers.Update(customer);
        await _context.SaveChangesAsync();
    }

    public async Task DeleteAsync(int id)
    {
```

```
    var customer = await _context.Customers.FindAsync(id);
    if (customer != null)
    {
        _context.Customers.Remove(customer);
        await _context.SaveChangesAsync();
    }
  }
}
```

Here, each method in CustomerRepository is asynchronous, using async and await to handle database operations. This approach optimizes I/O performance by avoiding blocking threads while waiting for database responses.

Asynchronous Programming in the Application Layer

The application layer orchestrates use cases, often interacting with repositories or external services. By making use cases asynchronous, you can ensure that application-level operations do not block resources, improving overall responsiveness.

Example: Asynchronous Use Case for Placing an Order

Let's implement an asynchronous PlaceOrder use case that interacts with a repository and a payment service.

```
public class PlaceOrder
{
    private readonly IOrderRepository _orderRepository;
    private readonly IPaymentService _paymentService;

    public PlaceOrder(IOrderRepository orderRepository,
    IPaymentService paymentService)
    {
        _orderRepository = orderRepository;
        _paymentService = paymentService;
    }

    public async Task<int> ExecuteAsync(OrderRequest request)
```

```
    {
        // Process payment asynchronously
        bool paymentSuccess = await
        _paymentService.ProcessPaymentAsync(request.PaymentDetails);
        if (!paymentSuccess)
            throw new InvalidOperationException("Payment failed.");

        // Save order asynchronously
        var order = new Order(request.CustomerId,
        request.OrderItems, DateTime.UtcNow);
        await _orderRepository.AddAsync(order);

        return order.Id;
    }
}
```

In this use case, both the payment processing and order saving are performed asynchronously. By making ExecuteAsync asynchronous, we prevent the application from blocking on either the payment or database operations, allowing other tasks to proceed.

Implementing Asynchronous Controllers in ASP.NET Core

In ASP.NET Core, controllers handle user requests, making them an ideal place to apply asynchronous programming. By defining asynchronous controller actions, web applications can handle multiple requests efficiently, even under heavy load.

Example: Asynchronous API Controller

Here's an example of an asynchronous OrderController that interacts with the PlaceOrder use case to handle order placements.

```
[ApiController]
[Route("api/[controller]")]
public class OrderController : ControllerBase
{
    private readonly PlaceOrder _placeOrder;
```

```
public OrderController(PlaceOrder placeOrder)
{
    _placeOrder = placeOrder;
}

[HttpPost]
public async Task<IActionResult> PlaceOrder([FromBody]
OrderRequest request)
{
    int orderId = await _placeOrder.ExecuteAsync(request);
    return CreatedAtAction(nameof(GetOrder), new { id =
    orderId }, orderId);
}

[HttpGet("{id}")]
public async Task<IActionResult> GetOrder(int id)
{
    var order = await _placeOrder.GetOrderByIdAsync(id); //
    Assume GetOrderByIdAsync is implemented
    return order != null ? Ok(order) : NotFound();
}
}
```

This OrderController uses asynchronous actions to ensure that HTTP requests are processed without blocking threads. This approach allows the web application to handle more requests concurrently, improving scalability.

Using IAsyncEnumerable for Streaming Data

With C#9, IAsyncEnumerable<T> allows you to stream data asynchronously, making it ideal for handling large data sets without loading everything into memory. This approach is especially useful for APIs or data-intensive applications that need to send data in chunks rather than waiting for the entire data set to load.

Example: Streaming Orders with IAsyncEnumerable

```
public interface IOrderRepository
{
    IAsyncEnumerable<Order> GetOrdersByCustomerIdAsync(int
    customerId);
}

public class OrderRepository : IOrderRepository
{
    private readonly ApplicationDbContext _context;

    public OrderRepository(ApplicationDbContext context)
    {
        _context = context;
    }

    public async IAsyncEnumerable<Order>
    GetOrdersByCustomerIdAsync(int customerId)
    {
        var orders = _context.Orders.Where(o => o.CustomerId ==
        customerId);

        await foreach (var order in orders.AsAsyncEnumerable())
        {
            yield return order;
        }
    }
}
```

By implementing IAsyncEnumerable, GetOrdersByCustomerIdAsync streams orders, allowing the application to retrieve and process each order individually, which reduces memory usage and improves performance for large data sets.

Handling Exceptions in Asynchronous Code

Handling exceptions in asynchronous code is crucial, as unhandled exceptions can cause unexpected behavior or crashes. Use try-catch blocks within asynchronous methods to handle exceptions gracefully.

Example: Exception Handling in Asynchronous Code

81

```
public async Task<int> ExecuteAsync(OrderRequest request)
{
    try
    {
        bool paymentSuccess = await
        _paymentService.ProcessPaymentAsync(request.PaymentDetails);
        if (!paymentSuccess)
            throw new InvalidOperationException("Payment failed.");

        var order = new Order(request.CustomerId,
        request.OrderItems, DateTime.UtcNow);
        await _orderRepository.AddAsync(order);

        return order.Id;
    }
    catch (Exception ex)
    {
        // Log and handle the exception
        _logger.LogError(ex, "An error occurred while placing the
        order.");
        throw;
    }
}
```

By handling exceptions with try-catch, you can log errors and provide meaningful feedback, enhancing application stability and maintainability.

Best Practices for Asynchronous Programming
To maximize the benefits of asynchronous programming, follow these best practices:

1. **Avoid Blocking Calls**: Avoid Task.Wait() or .Result, which block the current thread and defeat the purpose of asynchronous programming. Use await to handle tasks asynchronously.
2. **Use ConfigureAwait(false) in Libraries**: In libraries or non-UI applications, use .ConfigureAwait(false) to avoid deadlocks, especially if

the code doesn't need to return to the original context.

3. **Favor IAsyncEnumerable Over Task<List<T»**: When working with large data sets, consider IAsyncEnumerable for better memory efficiency and reduced latency.

4. **Handle Exceptions in Async Methods**: Always handle exceptions within asynchronous code to avoid unobserved exceptions, which can lead to unexpected application failures.

5. **Avoid Async Overhead in CPU-Bound Operations**: Reserve asynchronous programming for I/O-bound tasks. CPU-bound tasks can perform worse if made asynchronous, as they create unnecessary overhead.

Testing Asynchronous Code

Testing asynchronous code involves validating that asynchronous methods return the expected results without causing deadlocks or race conditions. Using xUnit, you can write asynchronous tests that use await to verify method outputs and behaviors.

Example: Asynchronous Test for PlaceOrder

```
public class PlaceOrderTests
{
    private readonly Mock<IOrderRepository> _mockOrderRepository;
    private readonly Mock<IPaymentService> _mockPaymentService;
    private readonly PlaceOrder _placeOrder;

    public PlaceOrderTests()
    {
        _mockOrderRepository = new Mock<IOrderRepository>();
        _mockPaymentService = new Mock<IPaymentService>();
        _placeOrder = new PlaceOrder(_mockOrderRepository.Object,
        _mockPaymentService.Object);
    }

    [Fact]
    public async Task
```

```
ExecuteAsync_ReturnsOrderId_WhenPaymentIsSuccessful()
{
    // Arrange
    _mockPaymentService.Setup(s =>
    s.ProcessPaymentAsync(It.IsAny<PaymentDetails>()))
        .ReturnsAsync(true);
    _mockOrderRepository.Setup(r =>
    r.AddAsync(It.IsAny<Order>())).Returns(Task.CompletedTask);

    // Act
    var orderId = await _placeOrder.ExecuteAsync(new
    OrderRequest { /*...*/ });

    // Assert
    Assert.True(orderId > 0);
}
}
```

In this test, await is used to handle asynchronous behavior, allowing the test to complete without blocking. By mocking dependencies, you can test the behavior of asynchronous methods in isolation.

Building a Real-World E-Commerce Application (Case Study)

I n this chapter, we'll dive into building a real-world e-commerce application as a case study to demonstrate clean architecture principles in action. This application will incorporate key elements of clean architecture, including domain-driven design, asynchronous programming, dependency injection, and testing. Through this case study, you'll see how the concepts we've covered come together in a cohesive, scalable, and maintainable solution.

Application Requirements and Design

The e-commerce application will provide a platform for customers to browse products, add them to a cart, and place orders. Additionally, the application will have a back-end administration system for managing products, inventory, and order processing. Here are the primary requirements:

1. **Product Catalog**: Customers can browse and search products, view product details, and check stock availability.
2. **Shopping Cart**: Customers can add items to a cart, view the cart, and remove items.
3. **Order Management**: Customers can place orders, and administrators can manage orders (e.g., update order status).
4. **Inventory Management**: Administrators can manage product stock and availability.

85

5. **Customer Management**: The system should manage customer profiles and order history.
6. **Payment Integration**: The application should integrate with a payment gateway for processing payments securely.

Based on these requirements, we'll define the structure of the application according to clean architecture, organizing it into core, application, infrastructure, and presentation layers.

Structuring the Solution

The solution for our e-commerce application will be divided into four primary projects:

1. **Core (Domain)**: Contains business entities, value objects, aggregates, and domain services.
2. **Application**: Defines use cases for the application's primary workflows, such as placing orders and managing the cart.
3. **Infrastructure**: Manages data persistence, external integrations (e.g., payment gateway), and other technical implementations.
4. **Presentation**: Provides the user interface (API endpoints) for interacting with the application.

Each layer will have a specific role, contributing to a clean and organized architecture.

Building the Core Layer

The core layer is the foundation of our application, defining the business entities, rules, and policies that drive the application's functionality. For this e-commerce application, we'll define entities like Product, Order, OrderItem, and Customer, and encapsulate essential business logic within these entities.

Example: Product Entity

The Product entity represents a product in the catalog, including its name, price, stock, and other attributes.

```csharp
public class Product
{
    public int Id { get; private set; }
    public string Name { get; private set; }
    public decimal Price { get; private set; }
    public int Stock { get; private set; }

    public Product(string name, decimal price, int stock)
    {
        Name = name;
        Price = price;
        Stock = stock;
    }

    public void UpdateStock(int quantity)
    {
        if (quantity < 0 && Math.Abs(quantity) > Stock)
            throw new InvalidOperationException("Insufficient
            stock.");

        Stock += quantity;
    }
}
```

The Product entity encapsulates business rules for managing stock. For example, the UpdateStock method adjusts the stock level while ensuring that it never goes below zero, preventing overselling.

Example: Order Aggregate

An Order is an aggregate that includes a collection of OrderItem objects. Each OrderItem represents a product added to the order, along with its quantity and price.

```csharp
public class Order
{
    public int Id { get; private set; }
    public int CustomerId { get; private set; }
```

```
public DateTime OrderDate { get; private set; }
public List<OrderItem> Items { get; private set; } = new
List<OrderItem>();
public decimal TotalAmount => Items.Sum(i => i.Price *
i.Quantity);

public Order(int customerId, DateTime orderDate)
{
    CustomerId = customerId;
    OrderDate = orderDate;
}

public void AddItem(Product product, int quantity)
{
    if (quantity > product.Stock)
        throw new InvalidOperationException("Insufficient
        stock for this product.");

    Items.Add(new OrderItem(product.Id, product.Price,
    quantity));
    product.UpdateStock(-quantity);
}
}
```

In this example, the Order aggregate manages the addition of items, enforcing business rules to ensure that products added to the order have sufficient stock available.

Building the Application Layer

The application layer coordinates workflows between the core and presentation layers. Each use case, such as placing an order or managing a cart, will be represented as a separate service, handling orchestration between different components.

Example: PlaceOrder Use Case

The PlaceOrder use case encapsulates the process of placing an order, including verifying stock, calculating the total amount, and saving the order.

```csharp
public class PlaceOrder
{
    private readonly IOrderRepository _orderRepository;
    private readonly IProductRepository _productRepository;
    private readonly IPaymentService _paymentService;

    public PlaceOrder(IOrderRepository orderRepository,
    IProductRepository productRepository, IPaymentService
    paymentService)
    {
        _orderRepository = orderRepository;
        _productRepository = productRepository;
        _paymentService = paymentService;
    }

    public async Task<int> ExecuteAsync(PlaceOrderRequest request)
    {
        // Create order
        var order = new Order(request.CustomerId, DateTime.UtcNow);
        foreach (var item in request.Items)
        {
            var product = await
            _productRepository.GetByIdAsync(item.ProductId);
            order.AddItem(product, item.Quantity);
        }

        // Process payment
        var paymentSuccess = await
        _paymentService.ProcessPaymentAsync(request.PaymentDetails,
        order.TotalAmount);
        if (!paymentSuccess)
            throw new InvalidOperationException("Payment failed.");

        // Save order
        await _orderRepository.AddAsync(order);
        return order.Id;
    }
}
```

The PlaceOrder use case manages the process of creating an order, adding items, verifying stock, processing payment, and saving the order to the repository. Each task is performed asynchronously to ensure efficient resource utilization.

Building the Infrastructure Layer

The infrastructure layer provides implementations for data persistence and external integrations, including payment processing and product catalog management.

Example: Payment Integration

To integrate with a payment gateway, we'll define an interface in the application layer (IPaymentService) and implement it in the infrastructure layer.

IPaymentService Interface

```
public interface IPaymentService
{
    Task<bool> ProcessPaymentAsync(PaymentDetails paymentDetails,
    decimal amount);
}
```

PaymentService Implementation

```
public class PaymentService : IPaymentService
{
    private readonly IExternalPaymentGateway _paymentGateway;

    public PaymentService(IExternalPaymentGateway paymentGateway)
    {
        _paymentGateway = paymentGateway;
    }

    public async Task<bool> ProcessPaymentAsync(PaymentDetails
    paymentDetails, decimal amount)
    {
        return await _paymentGateway.ChargeAsync(paymentDetails,
        amount);
```

```
    }
}
```

This approach allows the application to handle payments without being tightly coupled to a specific payment gateway, making it easy to swap out the payment provider if needed.

Building the Presentation Layer with ASP.NET Core

The presentation layer provides API endpoints for user interactions. Using ASP.NET Core, we'll build RESTful endpoints to expose functionality such as adding items to the cart, placing an order, and managing products.

Example: OrderController

The OrderController provides endpoints for placing and retrieving orders.

```
[ApiController]
[Route("api/[controller]")]
public class OrderController : ControllerBase
{
    private readonly PlaceOrder _placeOrder;

    public OrderController(PlaceOrder placeOrder)
    {
        _placeOrder = placeOrder;
    }

    [HttpPost]
    public async Task<IActionResult> PlaceOrder([FromBody]
    PlaceOrderRequest request)
    {
        var orderId = await _placeOrder.ExecuteAsync(request);
        return CreatedAtAction(nameof(GetOrder), new { id =
        orderId }, orderId);
    }

    [HttpGet("{id}")]
    public async Task<IActionResult> GetOrder(int id)
    {
```

```
        var order = await _placeOrder.GetOrderByIdAsync(id); //
        Assume this method exists
        return order != null ? Ok(order) : NotFound();
    }
}
```

This controller provides endpoints for placing an order and retrieving order details, interacting with the application layer's use cases.

Testing the Application

Testing the application involves verifying each layer independently, from unit tests for core entities and services to integration tests for repositories and controllers.

1. **Unit Tests**: Validate core entities like Product and Order to ensure they behave according to business rules.
2. **Application Layer Tests**: Mock dependencies to verify that use cases like PlaceOrder handle workflows correctly.
3. **Integration Tests**: Use a test database to validate repository implementations and ensure data persistence works as expected.
4. **End-to-End Tests**: Test the API endpoints to simulate real user interactions and ensure the entire flow works correctly from the presentation layer down to the infrastructure.

Performance Optimization and Profiling

P erformance is a critical aspect of any application, impacting user experience, scalability, and resource efficiency. In a clean architecture application, performance optimization and profiling help identify and resolve bottlenecks across each layer, ensuring smooth, responsive interactions and efficient use of system resources. Profiling provides visibility into how an application uses resources, while optimization focuses on refining code and architecture to improve overall speed and scalability.

In this chapter, we'll explore techniques for profiling and optimizing applications built with clean architecture, covering database optimizations, code efficiency improvements, caching, and asynchronous processing. We'll also discuss how to set up effective profiling and monitoring practices to identify issues before they impact users.

The Importance of Performance in Clean Architecture

Performance in clean architecture involves ensuring that each layer operates as efficiently as possible without compromising modularity, maintainability, or scalability. By identifying and addressing performance bottlenecks in each layer, you can create an application that handles high demand gracefully and provides a smooth user experience.

1. **Improved User Experience**: Faster response times lead to a better user experience, making the application more responsive and satisfying to interact with.

2. **Scalability**: Optimized performance enables the application to handle more users and larger data sets without consuming excessive resources.

3. **Resource Efficiency**: Reducing resource usage (CPU, memory, I/O) helps decrease operating costs and allows the application to run effectively even on limited hardware.

4. **Reliability and Stability**: Performance optimization reduces the likelihood of crashes or downtime caused by excessive resource consumption.

Profiling in .NET 5

Profiling helps developers identify areas of the application that consume excessive resources or take too long to execute. .NET 5 provides several built-in tools for profiling and diagnosing performance issues.

1. **Visual Studio Profiler**: Visual Studio's built-in profiler allows you to analyze CPU, memory, and I/O performance for .NET applications, pinpointing specific functions or methods that may need optimization.

2. **dotnet-trace**: A command-line profiling tool that captures performance traces from .NET applications, useful for detailed analysis without a GUI.

3. **dotnet-counters**: Provides real-time performance metrics, such as CPU usage, garbage collection, and exception counts, giving you insight into application health while it's running.

4. **Application Insights**: A monitoring tool that integrates with Azure, providing metrics, traces, and diagnostic information for cloud-based applications.

By using these tools, you can gather data about application performance, helping identify where optimizations are needed.

Optimizing the Infrastructure Layer

The infrastructure layer is often where I/O-bound operations occur, such as database queries, file access, and external service calls. Optimizing this layer can significantly improve the overall performance of the application.

Database Optimization

Database access is frequently a bottleneck in web applications, as it involves network latency, disk I/O, and query execution time. Some effective techniques for database optimization include:

- **Use Indexes**: Indexes speed up data retrieval by creating quick access paths to rows in tables. Ensure that frequently queried columns, such as foreign keys or search fields, are indexed.

Example: Indexing in Entity Framework Core

```
protected override void OnModelCreating(ModelBuilder modelBuilder)
{
    modelBuilder.Entity<Product>().HasIndex(p =>
    p.Name).HasDatabaseName("IX_Product_Name");
}
```

- **Optimize Queries**: Minimize the data retrieved by querying only the necessary columns. Use Select clauses to reduce the load on the database and decrease the amount of data transferred over the network.

Example: Optimized Query with Projection

```
var products = await _context.Products
    .Where(p => p.IsAvailable)
    .Select(p => new { p.Id, p.Name, p.Price })
    .ToListAsync();
```

- **Use Asynchronous Operations**: Perform database calls asynchronously to avoid blocking threads, especially in high-traffic applications. Asynchronous database calls allow the application to handle more concurrent users.
- **Implement Caching**: Cache frequently accessed data to reduce database

load. Tools like Redis or in-memory caching can improve performance by storing data in memory, reducing database calls.

Example: In-Memory Caching with ASP.NET Core

```
public async Task<Product> GetProductAsync(int id)
{
    var cacheKey = $"Product_{id}";
    if (!_cache.TryGetValue(cacheKey, out Product product))
    {
        product = await _context.Products.FindAsync(id);
        _cache.Set(cacheKey, product, TimeSpan.FromMinutes(10));
    }
    return product;
}
```

External Service Optimization

When integrating with external services, such as APIs or payment gateways, reduce latency by optimizing communication.

1. **Batch API Calls**: When possible, group API calls into batches rather than making individual requests, reducing network overhead.
2. **Timeouts and Retries**: Set timeouts and retries for external service calls to avoid blocking and retry failed requests, preventing long waits in case of a service delay.
3. **Use Asynchronous Calls**: Use asynchronous calls for external services to avoid blocking the main thread.

Optimizing the Application Layer

The application layer orchestrates workflows between the core and infrastructure layers. Optimizations here focus on asynchronous processing and minimizing redundant operations.

1. **Use Asynchronous Use Cases**: Implement asynchronous processing for I/O-bound tasks. For example, placing an order and saving it to

the database should be done asynchronously to maximize resource utilization.

2. **Avoid Repeated Data Access**: Fetch data once and reuse it within a workflow to avoid redundant database queries or API calls.

3. **Implement Caching in Use Cases**: Caching intermediate results in use cases that require repeated data access can improve performance, especially for complex calculations or data processing.

4. **Leverage Task Parallelism**: If multiple, independent tasks can be executed simultaneously, consider running them in parallel using Task.WhenAll to reduce execution time.

Example: Parallel Task Execution

```
public async Task ProcessOrderAsync(Order order)
{
    var updateInventoryTask =
    _inventoryService.UpdateInventoryAsync(order);
    var sendConfirmationEmailTask =
    _emailService.SendOrderConfirmationAsync(order);

    await Task.WhenAll(updateInventoryTask,
    sendConfirmationEmailTask);
}
```

Optimizing the Core Layer

The core layer contains the business logic, entities, and domain services. Performance optimizations in the core layer focus on efficient data structures, avoiding unnecessary calculations, and implementing lightweight entities.

1. **Avoid Heavy Data Structures**: Use lightweight data structures and objects, as the core layer is frequently accessed. Avoid excessive data copying or deep nesting, which can lead to increased memory usage and slower execution.

2. **Use Value Objects Carefully**: When using value objects, especially with C#9's records, ensure they are appropriately designed for immutability

and equality. Avoid creating excessive temporary objects within critical business logic.

3. **Optimize Aggregates**: When working with aggregates, minimize loading related entities unless necessary. For instance, when loading an Order entity, avoid loading all related OrderItems unless they are required for the current operation.

4. **Minimize Complex Calculations**: Cache results of complex calculations, especially if they are reused frequently, to improve performance. For example, in an e-commerce application, you might calculate a product's discount once and cache it, rather than recalculating it repeatedly.

Asynchronous Programming for Enhanced Performance

Asynchronous programming allows the application to perform multiple tasks concurrently, improving response times for I/O-bound operations. Using asynchronous programming wisely is key to enhancing performance:

1. **Apply async and await Properly**: Use async and await for all I/O-bound operations to prevent blocking.

2. **Avoid Blocking Calls**: Avoid using .Result or .Wait() on tasks, which can cause deadlocks and block the main thread.

3. **Use IAsyncEnumerable for Streaming Data**: Use IAsyncEnumerable for streaming large data sets, reducing memory consumption by avoiding the need to load the entire data set at once.

Profiling and Monitoring for Continuous Optimization

Performance profiling and monitoring allow you to identify bottlenecks and track improvements over time. Consider using the following tools and techniques:

1. **Performance Profiling with Visual Studio**: Use Visual Studio's performance profiler to analyze CPU and memory usage, identify slow-running methods, and optimize resource-heavy code.

2. **dotnet-counters for Real-Time Metrics**: dotnet-counters provides real-time metrics, such as CPU usage, memory, garbage collection, and thread activity, enabling you to monitor application health while it's running.

3. **Logging and Application Insights**: Log performance metrics using Application Insights (for Azure-hosted applications) or structured logging tools like Serilog to capture response times, errors, and resource usage.

4. **Automated Load Testing**: Use load testing tools like Apache JMeter or Azure Load Testing to simulate high-traffic scenarios and analyze application performance under load.

Implementing Caching for High-Impact Optimizations

Caching is one of the most impactful optimization techniques, reducing database load and speeding up frequently accessed data retrieval. Consider applying caching at various points:

1. **In-Memory Caching**: Store frequently accessed data, such as user profiles, product catalogs, or configuration settings, in memory to reduce database calls.

2. **Distributed Caching**: Use distributed caching (e.g., Redis) for applications hosted on multiple servers, ensuring that cached data is accessible across all instances.

3. **Response Caching**: Cache entire responses in the presentation layer, such as frequently accessed API responses, to reduce the time required for response generation.

Example: Response Caching in ASP.NET Core

```
[HttpGet]
[ResponseCache(Duration = 60)]
public async Task<IActionResult> GetProduct(int id)
{
```

```
    var product = await _productService.GetProductAsync(id);
    return Ok(product);
}
```

Best Practices for Performance Optimization

To get the most out of performance optimization, follow these best practices:

1. **Profile First, Optimize Later**: Always profile the application before optimizing. This approach helps you focus on actual bottlenecks rather than guessing where performance issues may lie.
2. **Apply Caching Wisely**: Cache only data that doesn't change frequently and clear the cache when data updates to avoid stale data.
3. **Use Asynchronous Programming Strategically**: Apply asynchronous programming for I/O-bound tasks but avoid it for CPU-bound operations, as it can introduce overhead without performance gain.
4. **Limit Data Access**: Avoid excessive data access by querying only the fields needed for specific operations and filtering data early to reduce load on both the database and the application.
5. **Continuously Monitor**: Implement logging and monitoring to catch performance issues early, before they impact users.

Deploying Your Clean Architecture Application to Azure

D eploying an application to the cloud provides scalability, high availability, and flexibility for your infrastructure. Azure, Microsoft's cloud platform, offers a range of services that complement a clean architecture application. In this chapter, we'll explore the process of deploying a .NET 5 clean architecture application to Azure, covering topics such as configuring Azure App Service, setting up Azure SQL Database, securing secrets, and managing application settings.

By the end of this chapter, you'll understand how to deploy and configure your clean architecture application to take full advantage of Azure's capabilities, ensuring a secure and scalable production environment.

Preparing for Deployment

Before deploying the application, review the following prerequisites and configuration requirements:

1. **Azure Account**: Ensure you have an active Azure account. You can sign up for a free account if you don't have one.
2. **Azure CLI**: Install the Azure CLI to manage resources from the command line, making it easier to set up and manage your infrastructure.
3. **Application Settings**: Define environment-specific settings (e.g., database connection strings, API keys) in a configuration file to ensure the application can switch between environments smoothly.

4. **Environment Variables**: Sensitive data, such as connection strings and API keys, should be set as environment variables in Azure, rather than hard-coded or stored in appsettings.json.

Step 1: Creating an Azure App Service

Azure App Service is a managed platform for hosting web applications and APIs. It provides features like scaling, authentication, and SSL certificates, making it ideal for clean architecture applications.

- **Create an App Service**: Start by creating an App Service in the Azure Portal or using the Azure CLI.

Azure CLI Command:

```
az appservice plan create --name
 myAppServicePlan --resource-group
myResourceGroup --sku B1 --location eastus
az webapp create --resource-group myResourceGroup --plan
myAppServicePlan --name myWebAppName
--runtime "DOTNET|5.0"
```

Here, myAppServicePlan is the App Service Plan that specifies the pricing tier, and myWebAppName is the name of your web application. The sku parameter defines the pricing plan, which you can adjust based on your application's needs.

- **Configure Deployment Settings**: In the Azure Portal, navigate to your web app, and under **Deployment Center**, configure deployment options. You can use GitHub Actions, Azure DevOps, or direct deployment via Visual Studio or FTP.
- **Enable HTTPS**: Under **TLS/SSL Settings**, enforce HTTPS to secure your application. Azure App Service includes a free SSL certificate for custom domains.

Step 2: Setting Up an Azure SQL Database

For data storage, Azure SQL Database offers a managed relational database solution with high availability, scalability, and automated backups.

- **Create an Azure SQL Database**: In the Azure Portal, create an Azure SQL Database. You can use the **SQL Database** option under **Create a resource**.
- **Configure Database and Server**:
- Choose a pricing tier (e.g., Basic or Standard) based on your application's performance requirements.
- Create a new SQL server, which will host the database, and configure an admin login.

Azure CLI Command:

```
az sql server create --name mySqlServer --resource-group
myResourceGroup --location eastus
--admin-user myAdmin --admin-password myPassword
az sql db create --resource-group myResourceGroup --server
mySqlServer --name myDatabase
--service-objective S0
```

- **Allow Azure Services and Local Access**: Under **Networking**, enable **Allow Azure services and resources to access this server** to allow your App Service to communicate with the database. You may also want to configure firewall rules to allow your local IP for testing.
- **Connection String**: Retrieve the database connection string from **Connection Strings** in the Azure Portal. This connection string will be stored as an environment variable in Azure.

Step 3: Configuring Application Settings and Secrets

Secure configuration management is essential for clean architecture applications, especially in production environments. Use Azure App Service's

Application Settings to manage environment variables and secrets.

1. **Set Environment Variables**: In your Azure App Service, navigate to **Configuration > Application Settings** and add the necessary environment variables, such as:

   - **Database connection string** (e.g., ConnectionStrings__DefaultConnection)
   - **API keys for third-party integrations** (e.g., payment gateways, email providers)
   - **Environment setting** (e.g., ASPNETCORE_ENVIRONMENT=Production)

2. Use Azure Key Vault for Sensitive Data: Azure Key Vault securely stores sensitive data, such as API keys and connection strings.

   - Create a Key Vault and add your secrets.
   - Use **Access Policies** to grant access to your App Service.
   - In the Azure Portal, configure **Key Vault references** in your App Service to access secrets.

Example: Retrieving Secrets in Azure Key Vault

```
{
   "ConnectionStrings": {
     "DefaultConnection": "@Microsoft.
KeyVault(SecretUri=https:
//myvault.vault.azure.
net/secrets/MyDatabaseConnectionString)"
   }
}
```

This setup allows your application to securely retrieve connection strings and API keys without exposing them directly in your application code.

Step 4: Deploying the Application

You can deploy your .NET application to Azure using several methods, including Visual Studio, GitHub Actions, and the Azure CLI.

1. Deploying from Visual Studio

- Open your application in Visual Studio, right-click on the project, and select **Publish**.
- Choose **Azure App Service** as the publish target.
- Follow the prompts to select your Azure subscription and App Service.
- Click **Publish** to deploy the application directly to Azure.

2. Deploying with GitHub Actions

- In your GitHub repository, navigate to **Actions** and set up a workflow with the .NET Core template.
- Add steps to build, test, and deploy the application to Azure App Service.

Example GitHub Actions Workflow:

```
name: Deploy to Azure

on:
  push:
    branches:
      - main

jobs:
  build-and-deploy:
    runs-on: ubuntu-latest
    steps:
    - uses: actions/checkout@v2
    - name: Set up .NET
      uses: actions/setup-dotnet@v1
      with:
        dotnet-version: '5.0.x'
```

```
  - name: Build with dotnet
    run: dotnet build --configuration Release
  - name: Deploy to Azure Web App
    uses: azure/webapps-deploy@v2
    with:
      app-name: myWebAppName
      slot-name: production
      publish-profile: ${{
secrets.AZURE_WEBAPP_PUBLISH_PROFILE }}
```

This workflow builds the application and deploys it to Azure App Service when changes are pushed to the main branch. Set the AZURE_WEBAPP_P UBLISH_PROFILE secret in GitHub to automate deployment.

3. Deploying from the Azure CLI

- Package the application by running dotnet publish in your project directory.
- Deploy the package to Azure with the following command:

```
az webapp deploy --resource-group
myResourceGroup --name myWebAppName --src-path
./bin/Release/net5.0/publish
```

Step 5: Monitoring and Logging

Once the application is deployed, monitoring and logging are essential for tracking performance and diagnosing issues.

- **Application Insights**: Enable Application Insights to monitor performance metrics, track errors, and analyze usage patterns.
- In the Azure Portal, navigate to your App Service, select **Application Insights**, and click **Turn on Application Insights**.
- Application Insights automatically collects metrics like request duration, response times, and error rates.

- **Logging with Serilog**: For enhanced logging, configure Serilog to send logs to Application Insights, providing detailed insights into application behavior.

Example: Configuring Serilog for Application Insights

```
Log.Logger = new LoggerConfiguration()
    .WriteTo.Console()
    .WriteTo.ApplicationInsights
(new TelemetryConfiguration { InstrumentationKey = "<Your
Instrumentation Key>" }, TelemetryConverter.Traces)
    .CreateLogger();
```

- **Monitor SQL Database Performance**: Azure SQL Database includes tools for monitoring performance, such as Query Performance Insights, which identifies long-running queries and potential optimizations.
- **Alerting**: Set up alerts in Azure Monitor to receive notifications based on specific conditions, such as high CPU usage, memory consumption, or error rates, ensuring proactive management of your application.

Step 6: Scaling and High Availability

Azure App Service provides auto-scaling capabilities that allow your application to handle traffic spikes automatically. Configure scaling settings to ensure that the application maintains performance under varying loads.

1. **Auto-Scaling**: Under **Scale Out (App Service Plan)**, configure auto-scaling rules based on CPU usage, memory, or custom metrics. Set the minimum and maximum instances to control scaling boundaries.
2. **Load Balancing**: For high availability, configure Azure Traffic Manager or Front Door to load-balance traffic between multiple instances, providing fault tolerance and geographic distribution.
3. **Database Scaling**: If the SQL database becomes a bottleneck, consider scaling it to a higher pricing tier or sharding data across multiple

databases for load distribution.

Best Practices for Azure Deployment

To maximize the benefits of deploying to Azure, follow these best practices:

1. **Separate Environments**: Use separate Azure resources for development, staging, and production environments. Configure App Service slots for staging to test deployments before promoting them to production.

2. **Use Managed Identities**: Enable managed identities for secure access to Azure resources without storing credentials.

3. **Secure Your Configuration**: Use Key Vault to securely store sensitive data, and restrict access through Access Policies.

4. **Automate Deployment**: Use CI/CD pipelines with GitHub Actions, Azure DevOps, or other tools to automate deployment, enabling fast and reliable updates.

5. **Monitor Regularly**: Continuously monitor application performance, set up alerts, and review logs to ensure the application remains responsive and reliable.

Scaling and Evolving Your Clean Architecture Solution

Scaling and evolving an application involves both technical and architectural considerations, ensuring that the solution can handle growing user demands, larger data volumes, and changing requirements. In a clean architecture solution, scaling is supported by modularity and separation of concerns, which make it easier to adjust individual layers without disrupting the entire system.

In this chapter, we'll explore strategies for scaling each layer of a clean architecture application and adapting it over time. We'll cover scaling techniques for the core, application, infrastructure, and presentation layers, as well as patterns and practices for evolving the solution to meet changing business needs.

Scaling the Core Layer

The core layer is responsible for defining the business logic and domain entities, and it should be kept lightweight and independent of external dependencies. Scaling this layer typically focuses on optimizing domain models and ensuring that business rules are enforced effectively as the application grows.

- **Optimize Domain Models**: As business requirements evolve, refactor domain models to support new functionalities. Consider using aggregates and value objects to simplify complex models and reduce

.dependencies.

- **Introduce Domain Events**: Use domain events to decouple different parts of the core layer. For instance, if placing an order triggers inventory adjustments, use a domain event to communicate this change. This approach allows the core layer to handle new business requirements without creating tight coupling between different domain components.

Example: Domain Event for OrderPlaced

```
public class OrderPlaced : IDomainEvent
{
    public int OrderId { get; }
    public OrderPlaced(int orderId) => OrderId = orderId;
}
```

- **Apply Domain-Driven Design (DDD) Principles**: Refine the core layer using DDD techniques, such as bounded contexts, aggregates, and entities, to clarify domain boundaries and isolate complex business logic. Breaking the domain down into bounded contexts ensures that each part of the application has a clear responsibility and can evolve independently.
- **Use CQRS for Command-Query Separation**: For complex applications, implementing Command Query Responsibility Segregation (CQRS) allows you to scale read and write operations independently. Use cases can be split into commands (for modifying data) and queries (for reading data), improving scalability by optimizing each type of operation individually.

Scaling the Application Layer

The application layer orchestrates use cases and application workflows. Scaling this layer involves ensuring that workflows can handle an increasing number of concurrent operations and that each use case can process data efficiently.

- **Implement Asynchronous Processing**: Use asynchronous programming for I/O-bound operations in use cases. For example, when handling multiple operations within a workflow, asynchronous calls allow the application layer to handle more requests concurrently, improving scalability.
- **Use Mediators for Workflow Decoupling**: Use the mediator pattern (e.g., MediatR in .NET) to manage workflows. Mediators allow different use cases to communicate without direct dependencies, making it easier to add or modify use cases independently.

Example: Using MediatR for Commands and Queries

```
public class PlaceOrderHandler :
IRequestHandler<PlaceOrderCommand, int>
{
    private readonly IOrderRepository _orderRepository;

    public PlaceOrderHandler(IOrderRepository orderRepository)
    {
        _orderRepository = orderRepository;
    }

    public async Task<int> Handle(PlaceOrderCommand request,
    CancellationToken cancellationToken)
    {
        var orderId = await
        _orderRepository.AddAsync(request.Order);
        return orderId;
    }
}
```

- **Cache Expensive Operations**: For use cases that rely on frequently accessed data, implement caching to reduce load on the application layer. For instance, cache product details or user profiles to avoid redundant database queries. Use caching strategies such as in-memory caching or distributed caching (e.g., Redis) for data shared across instances.

111

- **Implement Load Balancing for High-Traffic Operations**: When the application layer must handle high volumes of requests, use load balancing to distribute requests across multiple servers. With cloud services, load balancing can be automatically configured, allowing you to scale horizontally by adding more instances as needed.

Scaling the Infrastructure Layer

The infrastructure layer manages data storage, external integrations, and system-level operations. Scaling the infrastructure layer often involves optimizing database performance, implementing caching, and decoupling external integrations.

- **Optimize Database Performance**: Ensure that database tables are indexed for efficient data retrieval, particularly on columns used in search or filtering operations. Use query profiling tools to identify and optimize slow queries.
- **Implement Distributed Caching**: Use distributed caching to reduce load on the database. By caching frequently accessed data, such as product details or configuration settings, you can improve response times and reduce the number of queries required. Redis and Azure Cache for Redis are popular options for distributed caching.
- **Decouple with Messaging Queues**: For time-consuming operations, such as sending notifications or processing payments, use messaging queues to handle tasks asynchronously. Services like Azure Service Bus or RabbitMQ allow you to queue operations, enabling the application to continue processing requests without waiting for each task to complete.

Example: Queueing an Order Notification

```
public class OrderNotificationService
{
    private readonly IQueueService _queueService;
```

```
public async Task NotifyOrderAsync(Order order)
{
    await _queueService.EnqueueAsync("order_notifications",
    order);
}
}
```

- **Leverage Cloud Databases for Horizontal Scaling**: For high-traffic applications, consider cloud databases that support horizontal scaling, such as Azure SQL Database or Cosmos DB. These databases are designed to handle large amounts of data and can scale automatically based on load.

Scaling the Presentation Layer

The presentation layer provides the interface for users to interact with the application, making it crucial to optimize for speed, scalability, and a smooth user experience.

- **Use API Gateways**: API gateways help route requests to different microservices, aggregate responses, and enforce policies like rate limiting or authentication. They provide a central point of entry, which allows you to manage and scale API services effectively.
- **Optimize API Endpoints**: Optimize endpoints by reducing payload size, using pagination for large datasets, and limiting the data returned to only what's necessary. Minimizing response times ensures the application can handle more requests simultaneously.
- **Implement Response Caching**: Use response caching for endpoints that return frequently requested data, such as product catalogs or static pages. Cached responses reduce the load on the server and improve response times for end users.

Example: Response Caching in ASP.NET Core

```
[HttpGet]
[ResponseCache(Duration = 60, Location =
ResponseCacheLocation.Client)]
public async Task<IActionResult> GetProductList()
{
    var products = await _productService.GetProductsAsync();
    return Ok(products);
}
```

- **Leverage CDN for Static Assets**: Use a Content Delivery Network (CDN) to serve static assets (e.g., images, CSS, JavaScript) from edge locations closer to users. This reduces load on the main server and speeds up asset delivery, improving the overall user experience.

Evolving the Solution with Microservices

As the application grows, you may need to split it into microservices to improve scalability and development flexibility. Microservices allow each component to be scaled independently, optimized for specific workloads, and deployed separately.

1. **Identify Boundaries for Microservices**: Use domain-driven design (DDD) principles to identify bounded contexts, which represent natural divisions within the domain. Each bounded context can be separated into its own microservice, such as an **Order Service, Inventory Service**, or **User Service**.

2. **Use Message Queues for Communication**: Decouple microservices by using message queues (e.g., Azure Service Bus, RabbitMQ) for asynchronous communication. Events such as OrderPlaced or InventoryUpdated can be published to notify other services of changes without direct dependencies.

3. **Handle Data Consistency**: For data consistency across microservices, implement eventual consistency and use distributed transactions sparingly. Consider using a Saga pattern or transaction management

strategies to coordinate operations across services without relying on a central database.

4. **Automate Microservice Deployment with Containers**: Use containerization tools like Docker to package microservices, making deployment consistent and easily reproducible. Kubernetes can help orchestrate containers, providing auto-scaling, load balancing, and fault tolerance for your microservices architecture.

Using Event Sourcing and CQRS for Complex Data

Event sourcing is a pattern where state changes are stored as a sequence of events, which can be replayed to rebuild the current state. This approach, combined with CQRS, can help scale complex applications by separating read and write models and optimizing each independently.

1. **Implement Event Sourcing for Data Integrity**: Store each change in the system as an event, allowing you to replay events to restore state if needed. For example, each step in the order process (order created, payment received, order shipped) can be stored as an event in an event store.

2. **Separate Read and Write Models with CQRS**: With CQRS, you can optimize the read model for query performance and the write model for command handling. This allows you to scale each model based on specific needs, such as optimizing read models for reporting while focusing write models on data integrity.

3. **Eventual Consistency**: Use eventual consistency in distributed systems where immediate consistency is not required. This approach ensures data is eventually synchronized across services without locking resources, making it ideal for high-availability systems.

Monitoring and Scaling with Cloud Services

Cloud platforms like Azure provide tools for monitoring and scaling applications, allowing you to respond to changing load conditions quickly and effectively.

1. **Set Up Auto-Scaling**: Configure auto-scaling rules to add or remove instances based on CPU usage, memory, or custom metrics. Auto-scaling ensures that the application adapts to traffic spikes, maintaining performance without manual intervention.

2. **Use Application Insights**: Monitor performance metrics and track dependencies with Application Insights, which provides real-time insights into response times, exceptions, and resource usage. Alerts and notifications can be configured to warn of performance issues before they impact users.

3. **Implement Health Checks**: Set up health checks to verify that each component of the application is functioning correctly. Azure App Service and Kubernetes support health check endpoints that monitor the availability of microservices and restart them if they become unresponsive.

4. **Cost Optimization**: Regularly review resource usage and adjust resource allocation based on actual needs. Cloud platforms offer cost-management tools that help identify unused or underutilized resources, ensuring efficient spending.

Best Practices for Scaling and Evolving

To ensure a scalable and adaptable solution, follow these best practices:

1. **Keep Layers Decoupled**: Maintain separation of concerns to ensure that each layer can scale independently without introducing dependencies that slow down the application.

2. **Refactor Regularly**: Continuously refactor code to optimize performance, adapt to new requirements, and ensure the application remains easy to maintain.

3. **Implement Monitoring and Alerts**: Set up monitoring to track performance and resource usage. Alerts help identify and resolve issues quickly, preventing them from affecting users.

4. **Use Cloud-Native Services**: Leverage cloud-native services like managed databases, load balancers, and distributed caches to simplify

infrastructure management and improve scalability.

5. **Document Changes**: As the solution evolves, document architectural decisions, code changes, and configurations to ensure clarity and support future development.

Troubleshooting and Common Pitfalls

B uilding applications with clean architecture offers many advantages in terms of modularity, maintainability, and scalability. However, as with any architectural approach, developers can encounter common pitfalls and issues that may complicate development, hinder performance, or lead to maintenance challenges. Understanding these pitfalls and how to troubleshoot them can help maintain the integrity of your solution and prevent issues from impacting the user experience.

In this chapter, we'll cover common pitfalls encountered when implementing clean architecture, along with troubleshooting techniques and best practices to avoid these issues.

Common Pitfalls in Clean Architecture

Several common pitfalls arise in clean architecture projects, often due to misunderstanding core principles or overcomplicating design patterns. Let's discuss each pitfall in detail and examine how to avoid or resolve these issues.

Tight Coupling Between Layers

- In clean architecture, each layer should be independent and loosely coupled, relying on abstractions (interfaces) rather than concrete implementations. However, it's easy to introduce tight coupling by allowing dependencies between layers, which makes the codebase difficult to test and modify.
- **Symptoms**: Layers depend on specific implementations rather than abstractions. Changes in one layer often require modifications in others.

- **Solution**: Ensure that each layer communicates through interfaces and follows dependency inversion principles. Use dependency injection to inject dependencies, rather than directly instantiating objects.

Example: Refactor Tight Coupling

```
// Before: Tight coupling by directly creating a dependency
var orderRepository = new OrderRepository();

// After: Loosely coupled by injecting through an interface
public class PlaceOrder
{
    private readonly IOrderRepository _orderRepository;

    public PlaceOrder(IOrderRepository orderRepository)
    {
        _orderRepository = orderRepository;
    }
}
```

Leaking Business Logic into Other Layers

- Business logic should reside in the core layer to maintain separation of concerns. However, placing business logic in the presentation or application layers can lead to duplicated or scattered logic, making it harder to maintain and test.
- **Symptoms**: Business rules, such as validation or calculations, appear in controllers or use cases rather than in entities or domain services.
- **Solution**: Refactor business logic into the core layer, encapsulating it within domain services or entities. Use the application layer only for orchestrating workflows, not for enforcing business rules.

Overusing the Repository Pattern

- While repositories abstract database interactions, overusing this pattern or implementing generic repositories for all entities can lead to bloated code and performance bottlenecks. Repositories should be meaningful and focused on specific operations rather than handling every possible data interaction.

- **Symptoms**: Repositories contain generic operations with limited use cases, leading to complex query logic or difficulty in testing.
- **Solution**: Implement repositories only when they provide meaningful abstractions. For complex queries or multiple entities, consider using specialized query services or the Specification pattern instead.

1. **Over-Engineering and Premature Abstraction**
2. Clean architecture encourages modularity, but over-engineering or adding excessive abstractions can lead to unnecessary complexity, making the codebase difficult to understand and maintain. Avoid creating complex structures for features that don't yet require them.

- **Symptoms**: Excessive use of patterns, interfaces, and classes for simple tasks. The code is hard to follow, and development is slowed down by navigating complex abstractions.
- **Solution**: Use a "You Aren't Gonna Need It" (YAGNI) approach and build only what's necessary. Simplify code by avoiding excessive layers or abstractions for features that don't need them.

Ignoring Performance Implications of Asynchronous Programming

- Asynchronous programming improves performance but can introduce overhead if applied to CPU-bound tasks. Additionally, excessive or improper use of async/await can lead to deadlocks or increased resource usage.
- **Symptoms**: Performance issues or deadlocks in areas where async/await is applied to CPU-bound tasks.
- **Solution**: Use async/await only for I/O-bound operations, such as database calls or external service requests. Avoid using Task.Run for CPU-bound work and profile asynchronous methods to ensure they're

necessary and efficient.

Exposing Domain Entities Directly in the Presentation Layer

- Exposing domain entities directly in API responses can lead to data leakage and tightly couples the presentation layer with the core domain. This approach also makes it difficult to change domain models without impacting the API.
- **Symptoms**: Domain entities are directly returned in API responses, leading to exposed internal structures.
- **Solution**: Use Data Transfer Objects (DTOs) or ViewModels to structure data specifically for the presentation layer. Map entities to DTOs in the application layer before returning data to the user interface.

Example: Using DTOs to Encapsulate Data

```
public class OrderDTO
{
    public int Id { get; set; }
    public decimal TotalAmount { get; set; }
    public List<OrderItemDTO> Items { get; set; }
}
```

Lack of Comprehensive Testing Strategy

- Clean architecture facilitates testing, but a lack of well-defined test boundaries can lead to gaps in test coverage, making it harder to catch bugs or regressions. Without a clear testing strategy, it's challenging to ensure each layer is functioning as expected.
- **Symptoms**: Inconsistent test coverage, difficulty in isolating issues, and reliance on end-to-end tests for validation.
- **Solution**: Define clear testing boundaries for each layer, focusing on unit tests for core and application layers, integration tests for infrastructure, and end-to-end tests for the presentation layer. Use mocking to isolate

tests and minimize dependencies.

Troubleshooting Techniques

Use Dependency Injection to Manage Dependencies

- Dependency injection (DI) is crucial for maintaining loose coupling in clean architecture applications. If dependency issues arise, ensure that DI is set up correctly and that dependencies are registered and resolved in the DI container.
- **Troubleshooting Tip**: Verify that all interfaces are registered in the DI container. Use scoped, singleton, or transient lifetimes based on usage patterns to avoid issues with state sharing or unnecessary re-instantiation.

Profile and Optimize Asynchronous Code

- Profiling tools, such as Visual Studio Profiler or Application Insights, can help you identify bottlenecks in asynchronous code. Analyze tasks to ensure they're truly asynchronous and optimize any areas where async is misapplied.
- **Troubleshooting Tip**: Use dotnet-trace or Application Insights to identify slow-running tasks. Avoid using .Result or .Wait() in async code, as these can cause deadlocks and block threads.

Monitor and Optimize Database Performance

- Database performance issues are common, especially as data volumes grow. Use database profiling tools to monitor slow queries, and implement caching where appropriate to reduce load on the database.
- **Troubleshooting Tip**: Identify slow queries with database profiling tools like SQL Profiler or Azure SQL's Query Performance Insight. Use caching for frequently accessed data, and optimize indexes for efficient querying.

Check for Data Leakage in API Responses

- Data leakage can occur if domain entities are returned directly from API endpoints. Use DTOs or ViewModels to control which fields are exposed and ensure sensitive data is not included in the response.
- **Troubleshooting Tip**: Review all API responses to verify only the necessary data is returned. Use tools like Swagger or Postman to inspect responses for potential leaks.

Implement Logging and Monitoring

- Logging and monitoring provide visibility into application performance and errors, helping to diagnose issues more effectively. Implement logging across all layers and monitor application metrics in production.
- **Troubleshooting Tip**: Use structured logging frameworks, such as Serilog or NLog, to capture detailed logs. Configure Application Insights or similar tools to monitor performance metrics, error rates, and dependency failures.

Review Dependency Graph for Potential Cycles

- Circular dependencies can occur if layers reference each other directly or indirectly, leading to compilation errors or runtime issues. Review the dependency graph to identify and resolve any circular dependencies.
- **Troubleshooting Tip**: Use tools like Visual Studio Dependency Graph to visualize dependencies and detect circular references. Refactor dependencies into interfaces or separate services to resolve cycles.

Audit Security Configurations

- Security configurations are essential, especially for clean architecture applications that handle sensitive data. Ensure that secrets, keys, and sensitive configurations are managed securely and that API responses don't expose unnecessary information.

- **Troubleshooting Tip**: Use environment variables, Azure Key Vault, or other secure storage for sensitive data. Regularly audit API responses, configuration files, and environment variables to ensure that sensitive data is protected.

Best Practices for Avoiding Pitfalls

1. **Follow SOLID Principles**: Adhere to SOLID principles for each layer to ensure code remains modular, maintainable, and scalable.
2. **Encapsulate Business Logic in the Core Layer**: Place all business rules in the core layer, avoiding duplication or scattering business logic across multiple layers.
3. **Use DTOs for Data Transfer**: Use DTOs in the presentation layer to avoid exposing internal domain structures and maintain separation of concerns.
4. **Use Dependency Injection Consistently**: Ensure all dependencies are injected through constructors to maintain loose coupling and testability.
5. **Keep Testing Coverage High**: Implement unit tests, integration tests, and end-to-end tests, focusing on testing each layer independently to ensure functionality and prevent regressions.

Maintaining and Updating Your Application

Maintaining and updating a clean architecture application involves ensuring that the codebase remains organized, efficient, and scalable over time, even as new features are added, technologies change, and requirements evolve. Effective maintenance and updates not only extend the application's lifespan but also preserve its quality and usability, making it easier to introduce changes without compromising the original architecture.

In this chapter, we'll discuss strategies for maintaining a clean architecture application, focusing on code quality, dependency management, version control, regular refactoring, and handling technical debt. We'll also explore methods for rolling out updates in a controlled and efficient manner, ensuring stability and minimizing disruption.

Key Aspects of Maintenance in Clean Architecture

Maintenance is essential for a clean architecture application to remain effective and performant. The following aspects are crucial for successful maintenance and updates:

1. **Code Quality and Consistency**: Ensure the codebase adheres to consistent coding standards, making it easier for developers to understand and contribute.

2. **Dependency Management**: Regularly review and update dependencies

to prevent security vulnerabilities and take advantage of new features or performance improvements.

3. **Refactoring and Technical Debt**: Address technical debt and refactor code regularly to keep it maintainable and prevent it from becoming overly complex.

4. **Documentation**: Maintain thorough documentation to ensure that all changes and architectural decisions are well-documented for future reference.

5. **Automated Testing**: Use automated testing to verify that updates do not break existing functionality or introduce regressions.

Establishing Code Quality Standards

Maintaining high code quality is essential for ensuring the long-term success of a clean architecture application. Following consistent standards helps prevent errors, simplify debugging, and promote best practices across the development team.

1. **Define and Enforce Coding Standards**: Set clear guidelines for naming conventions, formatting, and code structure. Use linters and code analyzers, like **StyleCop** for .NET, to enforce standards automatically.

2. **Use Code Reviews**: Regular code reviews help identify potential issues, ensure adherence to clean architecture principles, and facilitate knowledge sharing across the team. Code reviews can prevent architectural drift and ensure that changes align with best practices.

3. **Static Code Analysis**: Use static code analysis tools, such as **SonarQube** or **ReSharper**, to identify code smells, potential bugs, and security vulnerabilities. Static analysis can also enforce best practices and highlight code that may need refactoring.

4. **Automate Code Quality Checks**: Integrate code quality checks into the CI/CD pipeline to automate code validation. This approach ensures that only high-quality code is merged into the main branch and provides immediate feedback to developers.

Managing Dependencies and Upgrades

Dependencies are an essential part of any application, providing libraries, frameworks, and tools that simplify development. However, outdated dependencies can introduce security risks and compatibility issues. Managing dependencies ensures that the application stays current and secure.

1. **Regular Dependency Updates**: Schedule regular reviews of your dependencies, including frameworks like .NET, libraries, and external services. Update dependencies to their latest stable versions, as these often include bug fixes, security patches, and performance improvements.
2. **Dependency Versioning**: Use **Semantic Versioning** to understand the impact of updates on compatibility. For example, a major version increase may indicate breaking changes, while a minor or patch update typically offers backward compatibility.
3. **Automate Dependency Updates**: Tools like **Dependabot** or **Nu-Keeper** automatically check for outdated dependencies and submit pull requests to update them, reducing manual effort.
4. **Manage Breaking Changes**: When dependencies introduce breaking changes, evaluate whether they align with the application's direction. Test extensively before making significant updates, and refactor code as needed to accommodate changes.

Addressing Technical Debt and Refactoring

Technical debt accumulates over time as shortcuts are taken or as the architecture becomes outdated. Regular refactoring helps manage technical debt, improves code quality, and ensures that the application remains adaptable.

1. **Identify and Prioritize Technical Debt**: Regularly review the codebase to identify areas with high technical debt, such as workarounds, overly complex logic, or duplicated code. Prioritize these areas based on their impact on the application's stability and maintainability.
2. **Refactor in Small Steps**: Break down refactoring tasks into small,

manageable steps to avoid overwhelming changes and reduce the risk of introducing bugs. Use automated tests to verify that refactoring doesn't break existing functionality.

3. **Focus on Core Principles**: Ensure that refactoring aligns with clean architecture principles. Simplify dependencies, encapsulate business logic, and maintain a clear separation of concerns to keep the code organized and modular.

4. **Set Time for Continuous Refactoring**: Allocate a portion of each development cycle for refactoring and addressing technical debt. This approach prevents technical debt from accumulating and ensures that the codebase stays clean and maintainable.

Documentation and Knowledge Sharing

Maintaining accurate documentation is crucial for knowledge sharing and ensuring that updates can be understood and implemented by different team members.

1. **Document Architecture and Key Decisions**: Create and update architecture diagrams, data flow diagrams, and decision logs that explain the rationale behind major architectural choices. This documentation helps new team members understand the codebase and allows for more informed future updates.

2. **Update Documentation with Changes**: Every time a significant update or refactor occurs, update the relevant documentation to reflect the changes. Ensure that documentation remains aligned with the current state of the codebase.

3. **Use Inline Code Comments Judiciously**: While clean code is often self-explanatory, comments can be helpful for explaining complex business logic or uncommon patterns. Use comments sparingly and only when necessary to clarify the code.

4. **Encourage Knowledge Sharing**: Conduct regular knowledge-sharing sessions, such as code walkthroughs or brown bag sessions, to promote a shared understanding of the application's architecture and encourage

collaborative problem-solving.

Implementing Automated Testing for Safe Updates

Automated testing allows you to verify that new changes do not disrupt existing functionality, providing confidence when updating and refactoring the application.

1. **Unit Tests for Core and Application Layers**: Implement unit tests for critical business logic in the core layer and use cases in the application layer. Unit tests ensure that changes do not introduce errors into essential workflows.

2. **Integration Tests for Infrastructure Layer**: Use integration tests to validate database access, API integrations, and other interactions in the infrastructure layer. Ensure that integrations work as expected, especially after dependency updates.

3. **End-to-End Tests for Presentation Layer**: End-to-end tests validate the entire application flow, simulating real user interactions. Use tools like **Selenium** or **Playwright** to automate UI tests and verify that the application behaves as expected from the user's perspective.

4. **Test Coverage and CI/CD Integration**: Track test coverage to ensure that all critical areas of the application are tested. Integrate tests into the CI/CD pipeline, running them automatically on each push to catch regressions early.

Managing Feature Flags and Controlled Rollouts

Feature flags and controlled rollouts enable you to release new features incrementally, reducing risk and allowing for testing in production without affecting all users.

1. **Use Feature Flags for Incremental Releases**: Use feature flags to enable or disable features based on user roles, environments, or specific conditions. This approach allows you to roll out features gradually and monitor their performance.

2. **A/B Testing and Experimentation**: For larger updates, use A/B testing to compare different versions of a feature with a subset of users. Measure key metrics, such as user engagement and conversion rates, to determine if the update improves user experience.

3. **Rolling Back Changes Safely**: If an update causes issues, use feature flags or deployment rollbacks to quickly disable the feature. This approach minimizes user impact and provides time to address the problem without compromising the entire application.

4. **Monitor Metrics for New Features**: Track performance metrics, error rates, and user behavior for new features. Use monitoring tools like **Application Insights** or **New Relic** to collect data and analyze the impact of updates.

Version Control and Branching Strategy

A robust version control and branching strategy is crucial for managing updates and maintaining a clean history of changes. Use a branching strategy that aligns with your development workflow and release schedule.

1. **Use Git Flow or Trunk-Based Development**: Git Flow and trunk-based development are popular branching strategies that allow for efficient feature development and integration. Git Flow uses separate branches for features, releases, and hotfixes, while trunk-based development keeps all changes on the main branch with small, frequent merges.

2. **Tag and Document Releases**: Use tags to mark releases and maintain a clear record of what each version includes. Create release notes that outline new features, bug fixes, and other changes for each version, making it easier to track the application's evolution.

3. **Review and Clean Up Branches Regularly**: Regularly review and delete outdated or inactive branches to keep the repository clean and organized. This approach also reduces confusion and minimizes the chance of merge conflicts.

4. **Use Pull Requests for Code Review**: Require pull requests (PRs) for all changes to the main branch. PRs provide a structured way to review

changes, discuss improvements, and catch issues before they are merged into production.

Continuous Monitoring and Observability

Monitoring application performance, resource usage, and error rates is essential for maintaining a high-quality application. Observability allows you to detect issues early and address them before they affect users.

1. **Set Up Application Monitoring**: Use tools like **Application Insights** or **Elastic APM** to monitor key metrics, such as response times, CPU usage, memory consumption, and error rates. Monitoring provides visibility into application health and helps detect issues early.

2. **Track Log Data for Analysis**: Implement structured logging with frameworks like **Serilog** or **NLog**. Log key events, such as user actions, errors, and performance metrics, to create a rich data source for debugging and performance analysis.

3. **Implement Alerts for Critical Metrics**: Configure alerts based on thresholds for critical metrics. For instance, set alerts for high error rates, memory leaks, or slow response times, allowing you to respond quickly to potential issues.

4. **Analyze Trends Over Time**: Use historical data to analyze performance trends, identify recurring issues, and proactively address problems before they escalate. Trends can help pinpoint bottlenecks and guide optimization efforts.

Best Practices for Effective Maintenance and Updates

1. **Adopt a Proactive Approach**: Regularly schedule time for refactoring, dependency updates, and addressing technical debt. A proactive approach ensures that the application remains maintainable and avoids the pitfalls of long-term technical debt.

2. **Use Rollback Mechanisms**: Plan rollback mechanisms for all major updates. This ensures that if a new feature or dependency update causes

issues, you can revert to a stable state without affecting users.

3. **Prioritize High-Impact Changes**: Focus on changes that improve performance, security, or maintainability. Prioritizing high-impact changes ensures that updates provide significant value and don't disrupt the application.

4. **Maintain Open Communication**: Keep team members informed about planned updates, architectural decisions, and code quality guidelines. Open communication reduces the risk of conflicts and ensures that everyone is aligned with the project's goals.